BIBLIOGRAPHIA OZIANA

L. FRANK BAUM

BIBLIOGRAPHIA OZIANA

A Concise Bibliographical Checklist of the
Oz Books by L. Frank Baum and His Successors

BY

Douglas G. Greene & Peter E. Hanff

Founded on and Continuing the
Baum Bugle *Checklist*

BY

Dick Martin, James E. Haff
and
David L. Greene

Published by
The International Wizard of Oz Club

CONTENTS

INTRODUCTION TO THE FIRST EDITION   9
INTRODUCTION TO THE REVISED EDITION   19

THE OZ BOOKS OF L. FRANK BAUM

I.	*The Wonderful Wizard of Oz* *The New Wizard of Oz*	25
II.	*The Marvelous Land of Oz* *The Land of Oz*	45
III.	*Ozma of Oz*	50
IV.	*Dorothy and the Wizard in Oz*	53
V.	*The Road to Oz*	57
VI.	*The Emerald City of Oz*	61
VII.	*The Patchwork Girl of Oz*	63
VIII.	*Tik-Tok of Oz*	66
IX.	*The Scarecrow of Oz*	68
X.	*Rinkitink in Oz*	70
XI.	*The Lost Princess of Oz*	71
XII.	*The Tin Woodman of Oz*	73
XIII.	*The Magic of Oz*	74
XIV.	*Glinda of Oz*	76
Addenda		
	The Woggle-Bug Book	78
	The Visitors from Oz	80
	The Third Book of Oz	81
	The Little Wizard Series	82
	Little Wizard Stories of Oz	85

THE OZ BOOKS OF RUTH PLUMLY THOMPSON

XV.	*The Royal Book of Oz*	87
XVI.	*Kabumpo in Oz*	88
XVII.	*The Cowardly Lion of Oz*	89
XVIII.	*Grampa in Oz*	90
XIX.	*The Lost King of Oz*	92
XX.	*The Hungry Tiger of Oz*	93
XXI.	*The Gnome King of Oz*	94
XXII.	*The Giant Horse of Oz*	94

XXIII.	Jack Pumpkinhead of Oz	95
XXIV.	The Yellow Knight of Oz	96
XXV.	Pirates in Oz	97
XXVI.	The Purple Prince of Oz	98
XXVII.	Ojo in Oz	99
XXVIII.	Speedy in Oz	99
XXIX.	The Wishing Horse of Oz	100
XXX.	Captain Salt in Oz	101
XXXI.	Handy Mandy in Oz	102
XXXII.	The Silver Princess in Oz	102
XXXIII.	Ozoplaning with the Wizard of Oz	103

Addenda

| | Yankee in Oz | 105 |
| | The Enchanted Island of Oz | 107 |

THE OZ BOOKS OF JOHN R. NEILL

XXXIV.	The Wonder City of Oz	108
XXXV.	The Scalawagons of Oz	109
XXXVI.	Lucky Bucky in Oz	110

Addendum

| | The Oz Toy Book | 112 |

THE OZ BOOKS OF JACK SNOW

| XXXVII. | The Magical Mimics in Oz | 114 |
| XXXVIII. | The Shaggy Man of Oz | 115 |

Addendum

| | Who's Who in Oz | 117 |

THE OZ BOOK OF RACHEL R. COSGROVE

| XXXIX. | The Hidden Valley of Oz | 118 |

THE OZ BOOKS OF ELOISE JARVIS McGRAW AND LAUREN
McGRAW WAGNER

| XL. | Merry Go Round in Oz | 119 |

Addendum

| | The Forbidden Fountain of Oz | 121 |

THE OZ BOOK OF DICK MARTIN
       The Ozmapolitan of Oz   122

CURIOSA

W.W. Denslow
     Pictures from The Wonderful Wizard of Oz   124
     Denslow's Scarecrow and The Tin-Man   125
     Denslow's Scarecrow and The Tin-Man and   127
         Other Stories
Frank [Joslyn] Baum
     The Laughing Dragon of Oz   129
Alexander Volkov
     The Wooden Soldiers of Oz   131
     Yellow Fog Over Oz   131

APPENDIX 1

Authorized Adaptations and
     Abridgments of the Oz Books   133

APPENDIX 2

Some Later Dust-Jacket and Cover Designs
     of the Oz Series   138

ILLUSTRATIONS

Photographs of all first-state covers and of most significant later covers of the books described in this checklist (including addenda and curiosa titles) appear in separate gatherings following page 64. Photographs of first-state dust jackets are included if they differ significantly from the cover designs.

INTRODUCTION TO THE FIRST EDITION

Bibliographies and checklists are generally tentative efforts to describe the publishing histories of certain books. So many variables exist in the publishing industry that despite the most thorough study and comparison of many copies of each title, some variants will probably be missed. The authors of *Bibliographia Oziana* have had the opportunity to consider much information that was unavailable when the checklist of first and early states of the Oz books appeared in *The Baum Bugle* from Christmas 1963 through Autumn 1968. The new material has required revision and expansion of the checklist, and we are fully conscious that additional information will be discovered by those who use *Bibliographia Oziana.* We hope, of course, that further evidence will confirm and amplify the sketchy history of the Oz books presented here, but in some instances new interpretations will probably be required. *The Baum Bugle* will serve as a clearing house for such new information and re-interpretation.

The plan of *Bibliographia Oziana* is to give a concise, descriptive publishing history of the Oz books. For *The Wonderful Wizard of Oz,* we describe all the major states until the type was reset shortly after 1920. For most of the other Oz books by L. Frank Baum, we include full details on copies printed up to 1919, when the publisher changed its name from Reilly & Britton to Reilly & Lee. Later copies are mentioned briefly. Only the first states of the Oz books by Baum's successors are described in detail. What precisely constitutes an Oz book is difficult logically to determine. We include descriptions of the forty books which scholars, collectors, and enthusiasts have generally considered the main Oz series; except for *The Wonderful Wizard of Oz,* these volumes have essentially the same format and were published by the same firm, Reilly & Britton (later Reilly &

Lee). Some other books which are not part of the regular series seem to us to be correctly classified as Oz books and they are included in the following pages as addenda. *Bibliographia Oziana* concludes with a section of curiosa: Oz-related books by those not normally considered Oz authors. We have not included modern Oz pastiches.

Readers of this checklist should understand something of the practices of publishing and book manufacturing that affected the Oz series. The nation's changing economic situation was perhaps the greatest influence on the physical appearance of the Oz books. When *The Wonderful Wizard of Oz* was published in 1900, it was an unusually elaborate book with twenty-four tipped-in four-color plates, and two-color textual illustrations throughout. It had a color-stamped cloth binding case, and it was issued in a decorative dust jacket. The costly format of the book reflected the conscious effort of the author and the illustrator, L. Frank Baum and W. W. Denslow, to produce a children's book that would be as enjoyable to look at as to read. Striking and innovative format continued to be a major feature of the Oz books until the first World War. By that time, printing and other manufacturing costs had forced the publisher to publish new Oz books in less elaborate editions, and earlier titles suffered from some streamlining to reduce the costs of keeping them in print. (Indeed, *The Wonderful Wizard of Oz* was in print in its original format for only about two years; when it was reprinted in 1903 by Bobbs-Merrill it contained only sixteen color plates and had other changes.)

The elaborateness of the early Oz books contributed in another way to proliferation of variations. Each book was made up of a number of separately manufactured components, including text sheets, color plates, decorated endpapers, and binding cases. Each component seems to have been reprinted or manufactured individually as supplies diminished, and the possibility of jumbling various generations of components in the manufacturing process was high.

The frequent occurrence of jumbled components suggests that the publishers of the Oz books often must have ordered larger printing runs than were to be bound and placed on sale immediately. The George M. Hill Company, for example, had a large stock of components for *The Wonderful Wizard of Oz* on hand in 1902 when the company went into receivership. It is likely that Frank K. Reilly and Sumner C. Britton (both of whom had worked for Hill) followed the same practice. Thus a printing order might have consisted of several thousand sets of text sheets, color plates, and binding cases. Then, as an initial stock was needed to put on sale, the publisher would probably order the casing of a portion of the sheets. As that stock was depleted another binding order would have been made, and as stock of a particular component ran low it was reprinted. It seems that the binding case was the element of an Oz book most often manufactured, for variant binding cases frequently appear on the same state text sheets of a number of volumes. Another form of jumbling occurred when an earlier binding case was still on hand as a later printing of the text sheets began to be bound up.

  Bibliographia Oziana describes the original appearance of each title and outlines the major patterns of change in the publishing history of each book. No attempt has been made to record all observed variants because many were caused by accident of manufacture. A record of every known combination of the components of every book would be almost endless and would not provide an accurate bibliographical history.

  Although this is a checklist rather than a formal bibliography with elaborate collations and transcriptions, we have used standard bibliographical terminology and concepts. To aid readers who are unfamiliar with bibliographical terms, we provide simplified definitions. The concepts behind some of the terms are complex, and serious students will want to study the more thorough discussions provided by Fredson Bowers (*Principles of Bibliographical Description*, Princeton University Press, 1949) and by G. Thomas Tanselle ("The Bibliographical Concepts of *Issue* and *State,*" *Papers of the Bibliographical Society of America,* Volume 69, First Quarter 1975, pages 17-66).

EDITION: All copies of a book printed from substantially the same setting of type. Thus most of the Oz books are, in strict use of the term, still in their original edition, never having had their texts reset.* Copies printed from plates reproduced from the original setting either mechanically (sterotypes) or photographically (photo-offset) are classified as part of the original edition. We have followed this definition except for *The Wonderful Wizard of Oz* and *The Marvelous Land of Oz*. In these two cases the change in publisher or title seems significant enough to retain the traditional (though inaccurate) division by "edition." †

PRINTING: Those copies of an edition whose texts are printed at any one time. An edition might consist of printings by various processes. For example, the first printing might be produced from type, the second printing might be from plates from the original type, and the third printing photographically reproduced from the second printing.

ISSUE: A group of copies of a single printing of a book which the publisher has openly identified in such a way that the group may be distinguished from all other copies of that book. The change must be a major one such as substituting one publisher's name for another on the title page, binding case, or both, or a designation such as "Popular Edition" on the binding case. Changes made simply to correct errors in the book, to alter advertisements, to rearrange or delete illustrations constitute states rather than issues.

STATE: Any variant that is not consciously planned by the publisher to identify a group of copies of an issue or a single printing. Some changes, however, are so minor

---

*Collectors should thus be wary of the phrase "first edition." If they are searching for earliest copies they should attempt to find first printings, issues, or states. Bookdealers should provide enough information so that buyers can identify the specific item being sold.

† This designation has now (1987) been changed on *The Marvelous Land of Oz*.

that we do not believe that they should be classified as states. For example, broken or dropped type may have occurred at any time during a single printing, and such seeming signs of type wear may, in fact, be due merely to dirt on the printing plates. We record such information whenever it is known, but not as distinguishing points between states.

GATHERING: A large sheet of paper which is folded, trimmed, and sewn into the book to form a group of printed pages. Normally there is vertical stitching visible in the center of each gathering. Early editions of the Oz books most commonly have gatherings of sixteen pages. (In some bibliographies and checklists, gatherings are called signatures.)

RE-IMPOSITION: A readjustment of the standing type for full pages of text to modify the format of a printed gathering or gatherings. If, for example, the first state of a book is made up of sixteen-page gatherings and the second state contains thirty-two-page gatherings, the text has been re-imposed.

CANCEL: A new leaf inserted into a book in place of an earlier leaf, usually to correct errors or defects.

TIPPED-IN PLATE: A color plate attached to a page of a book by means of a thin line of adhesive.

BOUND-IN PLATE: A color plate which is conjugate with another color plate. The pair of plates is wrapped around a gathering or a portion of a gathering and sewn into the book.

CASE: The part of a book which comprises the front and back covers and the spine. The case may be cloth, paper-covered boards, or paper (often called "wrappers").

BOARDS: Cardboard, covered either with paper or cloth, used for the front and back covers.

ENDPAPERS: Sheets pasted at either end of the book between the binding case and the text. Inserted end-papers are those in which the paste-down half is conjugate with the free half, and thus the endpapers are not part of the front or back gatherings. Self-endpapers, on the other hand, are portions of the gatherings, and the two parts of each endpaper are not conjugate.

SECONDARY BINDING: A term used to distinguish between variant binding cases used on the same state text sheets. The later cover is called the secondary binding.

LATER PRINTINGS: A term of convenience to divide later copies of books from the earlier forms. At times the precise point at which we insert the term in the following descriptions is somewhat arbitrary, and readers may wish to ignore it.

Other concepts and terms are generally defined in the body of the checklist or are understandable from their context. There are, however, a few points raised on the following pages which may not be immediately clear:

COPP, CLARK ISSUES: A number of Oz books are known that are identical with the Reilly & Britton/Lee printings except that they have the imprint of the Copp, Clark Company, Limited, of Toronto. Three types of such books are known:

A) Those printed at about the same time as the first United States issue. Reilly & Britton/Lee printed *Dorothy and the Wizard in Oz, The Emerald City of Oz, The Patchwork Girl of Oz, Tik-Tok of Oz, Rinkitink in Oz, The Lost Princess of Oz, The Magic of Oz, Glinda of Oz, The Cowardly Lion of Oz, The Giant Horse of Oz,* and *Pirates in Oz* for the Copp, Clark Company. Many experts believe that there were Canadian issues of all Oz books between 1908 and 1931 (and possibly earlier and later). Probably a very small number of copies of each book was produced, for these Copp, Clark issues are rare.

B) Those printed in 1941 by Copp, Clark: *The Land of Oz, Ozma of Oz, Dorothy and the Wizard in Oz,* and *The Road to Oz.* They are on cheap paper with no color plates.

C) Those printed erroneously by Reilly & Lee about 1960 when the firm went back to some of its old printing plates. The plates for two books, *Glinda of Oz* and *The Cowardly Lion of Oz,* apparently had the Copp, Clark name on the title page; and thus Reilly & Lee inadvertently created new Copp, Clark variants. These books are easily distinguishable from early printings for they have the Reilly & Lee spine imprint and have no color plates. Instead of the original Neill designs, the dust jackets contain pictures by Dick Martin.

SPINE IMPRINTS: Reilly & Britton and Reilly & Lee used a number of different imprints on the spines of the Oz books. The following examples should be used with the descriptions in the checklist. The major imprints (B,C,G, and I) may vary from title to title, and these samples will not match exactly each Oz book issued during the periods in which they were used; variation is especially apparent in the earlier imprints. Dates are only approximate.

A) "THE REILLY & ⏐ BRITTON CO.", ca. 1904-1905. (This imprint has been seen only on the first two states of *The Marvelous Land of Oz*.)

B) 'THE REILLY & ⏐ BRITTON CO.", ca. 1906-1908. (Although *Ozma of Oz* and *Dorothy and the Wizard in Oz* abandoned this imprint after 1908, it was used on all editions of *The Marvelous Land of Oz* and *The Land of Oz* from about 1906 until the firm became Reilly & Lee in 1919.)

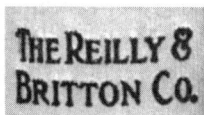

C) "Reilly & | Britton", ca. 1909-1918.

D) "REILLY & | BRITTON", ca. 1910-1912 and perhaps a little later. (This imprint is found on secondary bindings of the first state of *The Road to Oz*.)

E) "REILLY & | BRITTON", ca. 1914-1915. (This imprint has been seen only on the second state of *Dorothy and the Wizard in Oz*.)

F) "Reilly | & Lee", 1919. (This imprint, with the word "Reilly" measuring 7/8 inch in length, has been seen only on the first two states of *The Magic of Oz*.)

G) "Reilly | & Lee", ca. 1919-1933. (This imprint is occasionally called "boldface" in the checklist to distinguish it from later binding cases with the semi-script, "fancy" imprint.)

H) "Reilly ǀ & Lee", ca. 1923. (This imprint is known
only on the first state of *The Cowardly Lion of Oz*
and on ca. 1923 binding cases for *Kabumpo in Oz.*)

Reilly
& Lee

I) "Reilly ǀ & Lee" semi-script, "fancy" imprint, ca.
1934-1951. (This imprint first appears on the dust
jacket for the first state of *The Purple Prince of Oz*
[1932]; it is not found on binding cases of first
states until *Speedy in Oz* [1934]. This imprint appears
on later printings of Oz books well into the 1960s.)

Reilly
&Lee

COLOR PLATES: We give the locations of the color plates
in first-state copies. Later copies often rearrange the
plates, especially if a change has been made from tipped-
in to bound-in plates.

SIZE OF LEAF and THICKNESS OF VOLUME: Under
these headings we include the page size and the thickness
of the first state. These measurements can vary from
copy to copy depending on how the printer adjusted his
cutting machine, how tight the volume is, or how the
collector measures his particular copy. Thickness includes
the covers.

COVER: The color of the cover has been described from clean copies. The best method to determine the original color of the binding case of a faded or dirty copy is to examine the cloth on the inside of the spine. Unless otherwise stated, the spine stamping of first states is in black.

The description of each book begins with publication data: title, place of publication, publisher, date, number of pages, and illustrator. This material is not a direct transcription of the title page. The number of pages refers to the final page of the text; we have not included any illustrations, advertisements, and blank leaves which may follow the story, even though such pages may be numbered. Following the publication data is a phrase giving the number of states, e.g. "First edition, four states." This refers only to the early states which we describe; for many of the Oz books there are later states which have not been included.

The authors assume all responsibility for errors found in the checklist. We are aware that the scarcity of old children's books renders it difficult to examine enough copies of each title to be certain that all important variants have been noted and analyzed. Readers of *Bibliographia Oziana* will provide a service to the authors, to collectors, and to bibliographers and scholars interested in the Oz books if they will notify us of any errors or omissions. Corrections and further notes on the Oz series will be published in *The Baum Bugle*.

Although we are listed as authors of this book on the title page, in many ways we acted primarily as editors. Dick Martin, James E. Haff, and David L. Greene not only wrote *The Baum Bugle* checklist upon which this book is based, but they have also been closely associated with us on the current work and they have provided much of the additional information. Whatever merits *Bibliographia Oziana* may possess should be credited primarily to their assistance.

DOUGLAS G. GREENE
PETER E. HANFF

September 1975

INTRODUCTION TO THE REVISED EDITION

The corrections and additions in this revised edition of *Bibliographia Oziana* fall into several categories. First is the new material discovered since the publication of the first edition more than ten years ago. In the introduction (above, p.14), the authors speculated that Canadian issues published by Copp, Clark exist for all first-edition Oz books between 1908 and 1931. C.J. Hinke has now discovered such issues of all titles in the regular series between 1907 and 1931, except for *The Road to Oz*. These books are described on the following pages, but for more details readers are directed to Mr. Hinke's article, "Bibliographia Oziana: The Copp, Clark Story," *The Baum Bugle,* Summer 1981, or his book, *Oz in Canada* (Vancouver: William Hoffer, 1982). Marc Lewis has reported on first-state dust jackets for L. Frank Baum's Oz books ("The Dust Jackets of Oz," *The Baum Bugle,* Spring 1986). This material has been incorporated, in somewhat abbreviated form, into *Bibliographia Oziana*. Dust jackets for the Thompson and later Oz titles are not described separately because almost all of them fit a standard pattern: the paste-label design is reproduced on both the front and back of the dust jacket; the front flap has a plot outline of the book; the back flap has a list of Reilly & Lee Oz books. First-state dust jackets with unusual features, however, are noted individually.

Also in the category of newly discovered information is material on hybrid Donohue/Bobbs-Merrill copies of *The New Wizard of Oz* and several hybrid Reilly & Britton/Reilly & Lee copies of later Baum Oz books. In addition, this revised *Bibliographia Oziana* includes previously unrecorded colors for binding cases, especially on later Thompson and Neill Oz books, and changes in the approximate dates of printing of several variants. Moreover the late James E. Haff used Reilly & Lee catalogues to provide more precise dates for some late changes in the appearance of the Oz books. A point of clarification might be made here: around the early 1950s, Reilly & Lee occasionally used a boldface spine imprint in various sizes, similar to imprint G (p. 16), rather than the usual "fancy" imprint. An example of the revived boldface is shown in plate 27.

In the second category is the inclusion of books that did not appear in the first edition of *Bibliographia Oziana*. The Oz books sponsored by The International Wizard of Oz Club—*The Enchanted Island of Oz, The Forbidden Fountain of Oz*, and *The Ozmapolitan of Oz*—were written, like the previously described *Yankee in Oz*, by recognized Oz authors or illustrators, and thus are included on the following pages. Modern Oz pastiches and related volumes, however, remain beyond the scope of *Bibliographia Oziana*, but for readers interested in such books some titles are given on pages 129-130. The English translations of Alexander Volkov's Russian Oz books, *The Wooden Soldiers of Oz* and *Yellow Fog Over Oz*, fulfill the definition of "curiosa" and consequently they have been included. In the first edition, we decided not to describe Baum's *The Woggle-Bug Book, The Sea Fairies*, and *Sky Island* because, although they are about Oz characters, they "do not have the word 'Oz' in their titles and they do not take place in Oz." Ten years' consideration, however, has persuaded us that *The Woggle-Bug Book* is too closely related to the Oz series to be ignored.* *The Sea Fairies* and *Sky Island*, however, were part of Baum's conscious effort to break from Oz, and thus they will be described in *The Baum Bugle*'s current series, "Bibliographia Baumiana." Other books given bibliographical description for the first time include many later versions of *The (New) Wizard of Oz* in order to complete the publishing history of that book until 1956. We also provide additional details on British editions of *The (New) Wizard of Oz*. Interest has

---

*While this new edition of *Bibliographia Oziana* was in press, a book was published under the title *The Third Book of Oz*. It contains the texts of *The Woggle-Bug Book* and of Baum's 1904-1905 newspaper stories, "Queer Visitors from the Marvelous Land of Oz." A description of *The Third Book of Oz* has been added to the addenda following the Baum Oz books.

increased in the first adapted or re-illustrated editions of the other Oz books, and the significant versions are now described in an appendix. A second appendix outlines the dust jacket and cover designs used on Oz books since the late 1950s.

In the final category are changes that are the result of a thorough reconsideration of the conclusions presented in the first edition of *Bibliographia Oziana*. One problem that we decided cannot be resolved to entire satisfaction is the use of the word "state." In strict bibliographical parlance, a state is a change made to a portion of the sheets of a single printing of a book. However, both the Geo. M. Hill Company and Reilly & Britton/Reilly & Lee printed their books from stereotype plates so that individual printings cannot always be readily distinguished. Because many changes in the text of a book—whether the correction of a misprint, inclusion of later advertisements, or the reimposition of the text pages— could theoretically have occurred during a single press run (albeit as a stop-press change), we have designated such major changes as states even though it is likely that many of them actually mark separate printings.

The most important change in the description and bibliographical designation of an Oz book is our decision that all copies of *The (Marvelous) Land of Oz* printed by Reilly & Britton are part of the same edition. We previously had called the copies with the shortened title-page title the "second edition" (above p. 12). The change in the setting of a single page, the title-page, however, no longer seems to us major enough to warrant calling that state a new edition. Another change in the description of the second Oz book is a different approach to designating the various binding cases found on first and second state texts. Readers will also notice that a re-examination of what we previously called the first state, secondary binding of *The Emerald City of Oz* indicates that the volume represents a new printing of the text and the plates, and thus it is now described as the second state, with concurrent changes to the designations of later copies. The two forms of the contents of *The Little Wizard Series* booklets have also been re-interpreted.

The authors on the title page of any bibliography bear responsibility for the accuracy of the information and the designations, but in the case of *Bibliographia Oziana* they have been fortunate in the assistance of many others. Published bibliographical descriptions of the Oz books began with Jacob Blanck's inclusion of *The Wonderful Wizard of Oz* in his *Peter Parley to Penrod* (1938), Dick Martin's discussion of the same book in *The American Book Collector* (December 1962), and his further descriptions of the Baum titles in *The Baum Bugle*. James E. Haff, David L. Greene, and Douglas G. Greene followed with *Bugle* descriptions of the Thompson, Neill, Snow, Cosgrove, and McGraw titles. When the decision was made to publish *Bibliographia Oziana* in book form, Peter E. Hanff joined the project. Hanff and Douglas Greene decided to follow scholarly bibliographical principles and examined numerous copies of each Oz title, completely rewrote the descriptions of each book, and, while adopting the *Bugle*'s format, applied new, technical definitions of edition, issue, and state throughout. Haff, Martin, and David Greene continued to provide information and checked the written results at each stage, from typescript to proofs to published book.

The additions and corrections that appear in this revised edition of *Bibliographia Oziana* were written primarily by Douglas G. Greene, but once again with the help of the other authors on the title page. James E. Haff had annotated extensively his copy of the first edition, and through the kindness of John Van Camp his discoveries and observations are incorporated into the new text. Indeed, John Van Camp has acted for Jim in many ways, especially in keeping records on many variants. Douglas Greene prepared a series of "Working Papers" with the new information and reinterpretations, and distributed them among an ad hoc *Bibliographia Oziana* committee for comments. This committee consisted of the authors and John Van Camp, as well as the following who generously took of their time to provide assistance: Irene Fisher, Peter Glassman, Michael Patrick Hearn, C. Warren Hollister, Barbara Koelle, and Patrick Maund. In addition, valuable information for this edition was provided by Stanley Barker, Robert A. Baum Jr., Herman Bieber, Charles Boller, Henry Boudinot, Patrick Bowen, Jean Brockway, Russell Chappell, Bruce and Gail Crockett, Scott Cummings, Chris Dulabone, Jane Durgom, Nathan Faut, Michael Gessel, Eric Gjovaag, Alan Grossman, Jim Halacz, Tom Hemr, David Lee Hofer, Kathleen Johnson, Victor Kamhi, Rob Roy MacVeigh, Mildred Martin, David Maxine, Harry Mongold, Robin Olderman, Hugh Pendexter, Jane Pigney, William Rennagel, Richard Rutter, Justin Schiller, Dan Smith, David Stachowski, Steve Stringer-Smith, Amy Stubee, Milton Tack, George Van Buren, Lucy Washburne, and Paul Wilson. We are also grateful to C.J. Hinke and to Marc Lewis for allowing us to use the results of their research, and to The Bobbs-Merrill Company and to Contemporary Books (successors to The Reilly & Lee Company) for permission to reproduce cover designs of their books.

DOUGLAS G. GREENE
PETER E. HANFF

September 1987

THE OZ BOOKS OF L. FRANK BAUM

I. THE WONDERFUL WIZARD OF OZ

The first edition of *The Wonderful Wizard of Oz* has a complex format. It is made up of three separately produced components: the text sheets, the color plates (which include the title page), and the stamped binding case. The publisher apparently ordered a major modification of the text sheets after the first printing. The changes involved repositioning many of the text illustrations and correcting typographical errors. The color plates were also modified after their first printing. In addition, the binding case underwent several changes, the three most important of which are described below.

The modifications of the three components must have occurred soon after the first printing and before the original stock of text sheets, color plates, and covers was exhausted. Scrambled copies combining first and later states of the three components are often found. More complete descriptions of the book appear in Jacob Blanck's *Peter Parley to Penrod* (R.R. Bowker, 1938)* and in Dick Martin's "The First Edition of the Wonderful Wizard," *American Book Collector,* December 1962. Only the major points are mentioned here.

The Wonderful Wizard of Oz. Chicago and New York: Geo. M. Hill Co., 1900. 261 pages. Illustrated by W.W. Denslow. First edition, two states:

1. *Textual points*: Page [2]: the publisher's advertisement is enclosed in a box; page 14, line 1 has: "low wail on...";

---

*We describe in the checklist Blanck's first state Z. His state Y is probably a scrambled copy containing gatherings from the two major states.

page 81, fourth line from bottom has; "peices"; page [227], line 1 begins: "While Tin Woodman. . ."; the colophon at the end of the book is set in eleven lines and is enclosed in a box. Pictorial self-endpapers; the front paste-down endpaper is in black and gray, the back paste-down endpaper is black and red. The pages facing the paste-downs are blank.*

Color plates: 24 full-color, tipped-in inserts: title page and facing pages 14†, 20, 34, 36, 44, 56, 66, 80, 92, 102, 114, 126, [138], 150, 160, 170, 184, 198, 212, 220, 228, 246, 254. The verso of the inserted title page is blank or has a rubber-stamped copyright notice. The color plate facing page 34 has two dark-blue blots on the moon, and the plate facing page 92 has red shading on the horizon.

Cover: (Plate 1) light-green cloth, stamped in red and green on the front, back, and spine. The publisher's imprint at the foot of the spine occurs in one of the following forms:

A) In plain, unserifed type, stamped in green; the "CO." is set in ordinary fashion:

GEO.M.HILL CO.

B) Same as variant A except stamped in red.

C) In serifed type, stamped in red; the "C" of "Co." encircles the "o":

GEO.M.HILL ℂ.

*According to Blanck, first state copies have perfect type page 100, last line, and page 186, last line. Later copies have broken type in these places.
† Blanck reports that in some copies this plate faces page 12.

The green spine imprint (variant A) is associated with the earliest dated presentation copies. All later bindings apparently have red imprints. Variant B seems to have preceded C; variant C, which was used for an extended period, is the form most commonly found on later printings.

Dust jacket: Printed in dark green on pea-green stock. The jacket design is a monochrome version of the binding design. The publisher's imprint on the jacket is in unserifed type. The front and back flaps are blank.

Size of leaf: 8 3/8 by 6 3/8 inches. *Thickness of volume:* 1 3/16 inches.

2. *Textual points:* Page [2]: the publisher's advertisement has no box; page 14: "low wail of. . ."; page 81: "pieces"; page [227]: "While The Woodman. . ."; the colophon is reset in 13 lines with no box.

Color plates: The verso of the title page has a press-printed copyright notice. The color plates are the same as those of the first state except that the dark-blue blots have been removed from the moon on the plate facing page 34 and the red shading on the horizon has been removed from the plate facing page 92.

Cover: Usually variant C described above.

NOTE: Additional binding variants have been reported, but most differ only slightly from C. However, copies of a binding believed to be very late (as evidenced by plate wear) have been seen with the publisher's imprint on the spine stamped in red letters, similar to those of binding variant B. Another late binding, with spine imprint C, drops "THE" from the book's title on the spine.

THE NEW WIZARD OF OZ
Second Edition

Although they were produced from the original Geo. M. Hill printing plates, the early Bobbs-Merrill printings have several major changes, including a new title. For this edition, Denslow supplied new cover, title page, and endpaper drawings. Nine of the original color plates, including the original title page, were dropped. There are two states and a number of minor variants.

The New Wizard of Oz. Indianapolis: The Bobbs-Merrill Company, [1903]. Second edition,* two major states:

1. *Textual points*: Page 49: the illustration is 2 7/8 inches below the text. The text illustrations are printed in the following color sequence: red (pages [5]-111), green (113-144), red (145-175), green ([177]-222), red ([225]-[261]). On page 167, line 9, the words "yellow daisies" of the Hill printings have become "bright daisies", and on page 168, lines 2 and 11, the original "yellow flowers" and "yellow fields" have been changed to "scarlet flowers" and "scarlet fields". Inserted pictorial endpapers in green and orange. One copy, probably a binder's error, has been seen with blank endpapers.

   Color plates: 16 full-color tipped-in inserts, including a new title page. The other plates face pages 20, 34, 44, 56, 66, 92, 102, 114, [138], 160, 170, 184, 198, 228, 254. The copyright notice, printed in black on the verso of the title page, has been seen in two forms. Priority is uncertain.

   A) A single entry at the top of the page: "COPYRIGHT, 1899, 1903, | By L. FRANK BAUM AND W.W. DENSLOW. | *All rights reserved.*" The printer's imprint, in upper and lower case, is at the foot of the page.

---

*As the early Bobbs-Merrill printings have substantially the same setting of text as the Hill printings, they are technically part of the same edition, For clarity, however, we retain the traditional usage "second edition." G. Thomas Tanselle, whom we cite in the introduction, suggests that such printings created from earlier plates but by a new publisher should be considered "sub-editions." In which case, this is the first "sub-edition."

B) Two entries, in the middle of the page: "COPYRIGHT, 1899, | BY L. FRANK BAUM AND W.W. DENSLOW. | *All rights reserved.* | [rule] | COPYRIGHT, 1903, | BY THE BOBBS-MERRILL COMPANY". The printer's imprint appears at the foot of the page, in capital letters.

The captions on the color plates are newly set in an italic type that differs from that of the Hill captions most noticeably in the letters "*f*", "*s*", and "*y*". The caption on the plate facing page 56 omits a single quotation mark.

Cover: (Plate 2) dark-green cloth stamped in black and orange. The full title appears on the front cover and on the spine: *The New Wizard of Oz.* The back cover has an illustration of the Tin Woodman stamped in black, and the spine has a drawing of the Cowardly Lion in black and orange. There is a period after the author's name on the spine. The crow's eye on the front cover is in orange. The publisher's imprint on the spine reads: "THE | BOBBS | MERRILL | CO."

Size of leaf: 9 1/16 by 6 7/8 inches. *Thickness of volume:* 1 1/8 inches.

2. *Textual points:* Same as #1 except that the color sequence of the text illustrations has been changed. Gray-green (pages [5]-16) blue-green ([17]-79), red (82-96), green ([97]-144), yellow (145-175), green ([177]-222), brown ([225]-239), red ([243]-[261]).

Color plates: Same as #1 except that the copyright notice, printed in black on the verso of the title page, has three entries in the center, in slightly different type from entries A and B described above. "COPYRIGHT, 1899, | BY L. FRANK BAUM AND W.W. DENSLOW. | *All rights reserved.* | [rule] | COPYRIGHT, 1903, | BY THE BOBBS-MERRILL COMPANY. | [rule] | COPYRIGHT, 1903, | BY L. FRANK BAUM AND W.W. DENSLOW." The printer's imprint, in capital letters, is at the foot of the page. One copy has been reported as having the single copyright entry; others have been seen with the three-entry notice printed in black or in blue and without a printer's imprint.

Cover: (Plate 3) same as #1 except that the title on the front and spine has been shortened to *The Wizard of Oz*. "THE" at the top of the spine is in plain, unserifed type. Later copies omit orange from the crow's eye on the front cover and have reset lettering on the spine: "THE" at the top of the spine is in serifed type, and the period after the author's name has been dropped.

NOTE: Apparently no major changes were made in the book until 1913 when Bobbs-Merrill leased the plates to another publisher. However, the following minor variants of the second state of the second edition have been reported and are recorded in logical sequence:

A) The illustration on page 49 is raised to 2 5/8 inches below the text.

B) Type damage occurs on the top lines of page 169.

C) The running-title, numeral, and first two lines of text on page 169 a.e reset in a different type.

D) The "LIST OF CHAPTERS." heading on page [7] is in damaged type.

E) The illustration of the worried-looking lion on page [63] is printed there and is also substituted for the crying lion on page 68.

Because of the many components involved and because the book was kept continuously in print, copies may be found with one or more of the above variations present. The checklist authors will be interested in learning of still other changes.

Probably to secure British copyright, Bobbs-Merrill sent copies of its first printing to the Advocates' Library in Edinburgh, the British Museum in London (received July 29, 1903), and the Bodleian Library in Oxford (received August 13, 1903). The three copies differ from examples of

#1 found in America in that they have endpapers printed only in green.* The verso of the title page has the single-entry copyright notice.

Third Edition

In 1913 Bobbs-Merrill leased the printing plates of *The New Wizard of Oz* to M.A. Donohue, a reprint publisher. There are many Donohue variants, all of which fall into one of the major states described below.

The New Wizard of Oz. Chicago: M.A. Donohue & Co., [copyright 1903, ca. 1913 and later]. Third edition,† two major states.

1. *Textual points*: Similar to a late Bobbs-Merrill #2, with all of the type degeneration mentioned above, except that the correct lion is restored to page [63]. The colors of the text illustrations differ from those of Bobbs-Merrill #2: red, green, brown, olive-green, and yellow are printed without relation to the scheme of the story. The earliest reported Donohue copy has no additional resetting of type. Shortly thereafter page 14 was completely reset. Later copies lack the running title on page 44. Still later, pages 68 and 89 were reset, and the running titles on pages 44 and 49 were reset.

Color plates: The copyright notice (on the verso of the color-insert title page) is identical with the three-entry Bobbs-Merrill variant but without the printer's imprint. All 16 color plates (including the title page) are present. In earliest copies they are tipped in; in later copies they are bound in. The Donohue imprint replaces the Bobbs-Merrill imprint on the title page.

---

*Since the publication of the first edition of *Bibliographia Oziana*, one copy has been discovered in America with endpapers only in green. It also has the single-entry copyright notice.

† We retain the traditional designation rather than calling this version a "sub-edition."

Cover: Similar to the late Bobbs-Merrill #2 cover, described above. Various shades of green and blue cloth (one copy has been seen in light-brown cloth). The back cover illustration has been retained. The Donohue imprint replaces the Bobbs-Merrill imprint on the spine.

2. This state represents a severe cheapening in production.

Textual points: Color has been omitted from half of the text illustrations. Earlier copies have the textual illustrations on pages [195]-[261] in orange; later copies have these pages in brown. Apparently still later the picture of a witch's hat was deleted from page [137]. At least one late printing omits the color background from the Introduction page.

Color plates: All the color plates have been omitted except a double-faced frontispiece conjugate with the title page. The illustrations on both faces of the frontispiece vary; the following have been reported:

"This is a great comfort,' said the Tin Woodman."/"The Stork carried him up into the air." Some copies have this frontispiece printed in blue, light blue, and yellow; others have it printed in blue and yellow only.

"You must give me the Golden Cap."/"Permit me to introduce you to her Majesty, the Queen." Printed in blue and yellow.

"I am the Witch of the North."/"The Monkeys caught Dorothy in their arms and flew away with her." Printed in blue and yellow.

" 'I was only made yesterday,' said the Scarecrow."/"You ought to be ashamed of yourself!" Printed in blue and yellow.

Cover: The cover cloth is usually dark green, but several shades of green and blue have been seen. The back cover is blank. One copy has been reported with stamped white decorations on the Scarecrow on the front cover.

About 1920, Bobbs-Merrill regained the printing plates for the book and, presumably, remaining Donohue stock. Two

Bobbs-Merrill/Donohue hybrid copies have been reported, both with cover designs similar to earlier Bobbs-Merrill and Donohue copies. The spine, however, reads "Bobbs Merrill". The back covers of both hybrid copies are blank. One copy has the first state Donohue color plates and text with reset type noted above. The title page is similar to that of the second edition, including a Bobbs-Merrill imprint. The other copy has a late second state Donohue text (color omitted from half the text illustrations; no witch's hat on page [137]). The conjugate double-faced frontispiece/title page has been replaced with a type-set Bobbs-Merrill title page, printed on coated plate-stock and tipped in. The title page is printed in black, with a double-rule border in red. The word "New" from the title is omitted. Both of these hybrids contain the standard copyright notice seen in Donohue printings: three entries with no printer's imprint.

Fourth Edition

The New Wizard of Oz. Indianapolis: The Bobbs-Merrill Co., [copyright 1903, ca. 1920]. Fourth edition:*

Textual points: All the reset type noted in the Donohue printings is present. In addition, the "LIST OF CHAPTERS." heading on page [7] and the running titles on pages 222 and 234 have been reset. Page [137] has a crude re-drawing of the witch's hat. All the text illustrations are once again in color, but the color sequence differs from earlier printings: tan (pages [5]-[65]), yellow (68-129), green (131-[193]), red ([195]-[261]). The inserted end-papers are blank.

Color plates: Title page printed in full color, similar to early Bobbs-Merrill printings; the verso has an added line, *"Printed in the United States of America"*, above the

---

*Again we retain the traditional designation rather than calling this version a "sub-edition."

printer's imprint. The other 15 full-color inserts have been reinstated, with reset captions. There is a misprint on the last color plate: *"Cup"* for *"Cap"*. A double-page frontispiece precedes the title page; a black-and-white photograph of Fred Stone, and a letter from Stone, *"To My Little Friends:"*, facing it.

Cover: (Plate 4) green cloth, spine stamped in blue. On the front is a pictorial paper label printed in dark blue, green, and orange. The back cover is blank.

Fifth Edition

The New Wizard of Oz. Indianapolis: The Bobbs-Merrill Co., [copyright 1903, printed in 1920s-1930s]. 208 pages. Fifth edition, two states:

1. *Textual points:* The text has been entirely reset, and most of the text illustrations have been removed. The few that remain are in black and white. These changes result in a book of only 208 pages.

Color plates: 16 full-color inserts, including the title page.

Cover: Normally dark-green cloth. The pictorial paper label and the stamping are similar to the fourth edition. Some copies have tan or yellow replacing the dark blue of the cover label.

2. *Textual points, color plates,* and *cover:* Same as #1, except that this state contains only 8 color inserts; the other 8 of the previous state, including the title page, now appear as full-page textual illustrations in black and white. Some copies also have tan or yellow replacing the dark blue of the cover label.

While continuing to publish the fifth edition Bobbs-Merrill also made arrangements for the release of *The New Wizard of Oz* in two other forms.

1925 Photoplay Version

This version was published in conjunction with the distribution in 1925 of the Chadwick Pictures silent film, *The Wizard of Oz*, featuring Larry Semon as the Scarecrow, Oliver Hardy as the Tin Woodman, and Dorothy Dwan as Dorothy.

The New Wizard of Oz. Indianapolis: The Bobbs-Merrill Co., [copyright 1903, published 1925]. 208 pages.

Textual points: Identical with the fifth edition, second state.

Plates: 8 movie stills facing pages 14, 42, 58, 102, 118, 140, 170, 192.

Cover: (Plate 5) green cloth, stamped in lavender on the front and spine. There is no paper label. The back cover is blank. The book was issued in a pictorial dust jacket (plate 6).

No variants have been reported.

1934 Waddle Book

In 1934, Bobbs-Merrill leased its plates to Blue Ribbon Books, a subsidiary of Doubleday, Doran. This Waddle Book contains 6 die-cut "Waddle Toys" which when assembled would waddle down a sloping cardboard, yellow brick road runway which was enclosed in an inserted envelope held to the back cover of the book by a 4-inch wide decorated paper band. Copies with the Waddles are rarely found, and thus the states of the book are difficult to determine, but the following seems to be the pattern.

The Wizard of Oz Waddle Book. New York: Blue Ribbon Books, Inc., 1934. Two states:

1. *Textual points*: Similar to the fifth edition, second state, with the following changes: there is a new title page; an additional entry is included at the end of the contents page for instructions to assemble the Waddles; and pages [209]-[211] give the instructions.

Color plates and *inserts*: 8 color plates with text printed on the versos. The punch-out Waddle figures are printed on sheets of heavy card stock which are tipped to bound-in perforated stubs between pages 46/47, 94/95, and 143/144; the wraparounds of the stubs emerge at pages 55/56, 102/103, 150/151.

Cover: Light green cloth with a flat spine. The front has a new label showing the Waddles waddling. The spine has an imprint for Blue Ribbon Books at the foot. The back is blank.

2. *Textual points*: Same as #1.

Color plates and *inserts*: Same as #1 except that the Waddles are not attached to stubs but enclosed in the envelope containing the runway. The paper stubs, however, seem to be retained, at least in some copies.

Cover: (Plate 7) same as #1 except that it is light olive cloth with a rounded spine, and there is no publisher's imprint at the foot of the spine.

After the plates were returned to Bobbs-Merrill, some printings of *The New Wizard of Oz* continued to have the additional Waddle entry on the contents page. These copies, printed between 1935 and 1939, are bound in a much lighter green cloth than previous printings of the fifth edition. Several copies have been reported with text on the back of the color plates, as in the Waddle edition.

1939 MGM Movie Version

The New Wizard of Oz. Indianapolis: The Bobbs-Merrill Company, [copyright 1903, published 1939]. Two states:

1. *Textual points*: Same as copies of the fifth edition from the later 1930s, except that the erroneous Waddle entry from the contents page has been omitted and the book has inserted endpapers reproducing stills in sepia from the MGM movie, *The Wizard of Oz*.

Color plates: 8 color plates with black replacing the blue of earlier printings.

Cover: (Plate 8) light green or medium-dark green cloth, stamped on the front in black and on the spine in black and gold; the spine has black fields behind the printing. The back cover is blank. Issued in a pictorial dust jacket (plate 9).

Size of leaf: The book is larger than earlier printings; the page size is 9 5/8 by 7 inches.

2. *Textual points, color plates* and *cover*: Same as #1 except that the endpapers are blank and that there are no black fields on the spine. Copies have been seen bound in light green and in medium-dark green cloth.

The release of the MGM movie *The Wizard of Oz* in 1939 resulted in the first rewritten versions of the story. Because they do not contain L. Frank Baum's wordings, they are adaptations rather than abridgments. The following books are the first editions of the story to have pictures by illustrators other than Denslow.

1939 Adaptation Illustrated by Leason

The Wizard of Oz Picture Book. Racine: Whitman Publishing Co., 1939. 12 unnumbered pages, including the covers. [Illustrations signed "Leason".]

Textual points and *cover*. Made up of a single gathering, saddle wire-stitched (stapled in the center). The front and back wrappers (plate 10) are trimmed to page size and printed on the same textured stock as the contents, and the story begins on the verso of the front cover and ends on the recto of the back cover. The top three-fourths of each page contains a full-color illustration.

Size of leaf: 12 1/2 by 8 5/8 inches. *Thickness of volume*: 3/32 inch.

No variants have been reported.

1939 Adaptation Illustrated by Henry E. Vallely

The Story of the Wizard of Oz. Racine: Whitman Publishing Company, 1939. 48 pages. Illustrated by Henry E. Vallely. Two editions, one issued regularly, the other distributed as promotion for Cocomalt, a malted food drink. Priority is unknown.

A (regular edition). *Textual points*: Made up of a single gathering, saddle wire-stitched (stapled in the center). Page 12 begins "The".

Cover: (Plate 11) pictorial stiff-paper wrappers, trimmed to page size. The same illustration in color appears on the front and back covers. The figures fill almost all the space beneath the title; the Scarecrow is about 7 1/4 inches tall. The number "708" is printed on the bottom left of both covers. The inside of the back cover is blank.

Size of leaf: 10 15/16 by 8 15/16 inches. *Thickness of volume* varies as apparently different paper stocks were used, but it is approximately 1/4 inch.

B (Cocomalt edition). *Textual points*: Similar to the regular edition, but the text and captions to the illustrations are set in a slightly smaller type. As a result, although the book has the same number of pages as the regular edition, often the first word of text on a page differs. Page 12, for example, begins "By".

Cover: Similar to the regular edition, with the following exceptions: on the bottom of the front and back covers has been added "WITH PICTURES TO COLOR"; the number "708" is omitted; the picture is smaller (the Scarecrow is approximately 6 3/4 inches tall); and the inside of the back cover has an advertisement for Cocomalt.

Size of leaf: The Cocomalt edition is taller and narrower than the regular edition, approximately 10 7/8 by 8 1/4 inches.

1939 Adaptation Illustrated by Oskar Lebeck

The Wizard of Oz. New York: Grosset & Dunlap, 1939. 56 unnumbered pages. Illustrated by Oskar Lebeck.

Textual points: Made up of four gatherings, the first and last containing 12 pages each; the other two with 16 pages each. Wire side-stitched (stapled). Color is used in many of the text illustrations. The book contains pictorial lining papers (paste-down sheets), printed in blue, on the inside of the front and back covers, and matching pages facing the paste-downs to simulate endpapers.

Cover: (Plate 12) Pictorial paper-covered boards, with a blank blue-cloth spine.

Size of leaf: 6 7/8 by 8 5/8 inches (measured from the wire-stitching). *Thickness of volume*: approximately 7/16 inch.

No variants have been reported.

1944 Adaptation Animated by Julian Wehr

The Wizard of Oz. Akron: Saalfield Publishing Company, 1944. 24 unnumbered pages. Animations by Julian Wehr.

Textual points; Made up of six single leaves and six double-size leaves which are printed on one side and folded to provide for the parts making up the animations. All the leaves are held together and attached to the cover by notched, cyclindrical red plastic. Illustrations in color. The foot of the copyright page reads: *"Created and Produced by the* | DUENEWALD PRINTING CORP., NEW YORK, N.Y. | Sole Agent for *Wehr Animation.* Patent No.2192763 | PRINTED IN THE U.S.A.*" Self-endpapers printed in solid blue.

Cover: (Plate 13) pictorial paper-covered boards, with the same illustration on the front and back.

Size of leaf: Varies slightly but approximately 8 1/2 by 6 1/2 inches. *Thickness of volume*: 3/8 inch.

No variants have been reported.

1944 Edition Illustrated by Evelyn Copelman

In 1944, Bobbs-Merrill decided that the book needed a more modern appearance, and chose Evelyn Copelman to re-illustrate it. Though the title page says her work was "adapted from the famous pictures by W.W. Denslow," it is clear that the MGM movie was her main inspiration.

The New Wizard of Oz. Indianapolis [and] New York: The Bobbs-Merrill Company, [1944]. 209 pages. Illustrated by Evelyn Copelman. First edition in this form, several states:

1. *Textual points*: 16-page gatherings. The verso of the title page contains the three copyright notices from earlier full-length editions, and an additional entry: "COPYRIGHT, 1944 | BY THE BOBBS-MERRILL COMPANY". At the foot is: "PRINTED IN THE UNITED STATES OF AMERICA | BY THE CORNWALL PRESS, CORNWALL, N.Y." Page 193, 4th line from the foot, contains a misprint: "trmendous". Inserted blank endpapers.

Color plates: 8 full-color inserts, printed on text stock, tipped-in facing pages 40, 64, 78, 124, 138, 146, 160, 206. The plate facing page 64 (Dorothy in the poppies) shows Dorothy looking to the right of the picture; the plate facing page 78 (Dorothy and the field mice) shows Dorothy looking to the left of the picture; the plate facing page 138 (Dorothy and the Winged Monkeys) shows Dorothy looking to the right of the picture. Late copies of this state have the plates bound-in rather than tipped-in, and the placement has been changed.

Cover: (Plate 14) green cloth, stamped on the front and spine in black and gilt,and on the back in black. Issued in a pictorial dust jacket (plate 15).

Size of leaf: 9 7/16 by 7 inches. *Thickness of volume*: 15/16 inch.

Bobbs-Merrill frequently reprinted this edition, making many minor changes. The printer's imprint on the verso of the title page occurs in different forms; the order of the color plates was altered so that the Cowardly Lion drinks the courage toward the beginning of the book rather than near the end as the earlier printings correctly have it; some copies have 32-page gatherings rather than 16-page gatherings. In short, about ten states have been identified, but arbitrarily the following have been labelled as the major versions:

2. Similar to late copies of #1 with bound-in plates, except that the cover is blue cloth.

3. Similar to #2 except that the plates showing Dorothy in the poppies, Dorothy and the field mice, and Dorothy and the Winged Monkeys have been inverted so that Dorothy is now looking toward the other side of each plate. Late copies of this state correct the misprint on page 193. Most copies of this state are bound in blue cloth, but the final binding case was gray paper-covered boards with a red-cloth spine which extends onto the boards for about an inch.

4. Similar to #s 1, 2, and 3, except that it is in deluxe format, approximately 11 by 8 1/2 inches, and it is bound in light-blue cloth stamped in silver without illustrations on the cover. The 8 color plates are printed on 6 leaves; the first 2 and the final 2 are on single leaves. This state was produced in 1964, eight years after Bobbs-Merrill had allowed another publisher, Grosset & Dunlap, to use the Copelman illustrations (see below).

Around 1944, a Canadian printing was published by McClelland & Stewart of Toronto. It is similar to the first

Bobbs-Merrill state with the Copelman illustrations, and it has the misprint on page 193. It is bound in green cloth, stamped in red on the front and spine; the back is blank. The spine has the Canadian imprint; the title page retains the United States imprint, but adds the Canadian imprint beneath it.

In 1956, Grosset & Dunlap published an expanded edition illustrated by Copelman in its Illustrated Junior Library series, which has appeared in various formats. This version contains reset type. Some of the textual illustrations have been redrawn, and some new textual pictures have been included. It has 10 rather than 8 color plates.

Before the copyright expired on the book, Bobbs-Merrill contracted for three other editions, each with new illustrations. Two are adaptations (Random House, 1950, illustrated by Anton Loeb, and Wonder Books, 1951, illustrated by Tom Sinnickson); and one is full-length (Junior Deluxe Editions, 1955, illustrated by Leonard Weisgard). After the book entered public domain in 1956, many publishers issued printings of it. Especially noteworthy are near-facsimiles (some of the pictures are re-engraved) published by Dover Publications (1960), Crown (1961), Columbia Records (1969), and Clarkson N. Potter as part of Michael Patrick Hearn's *The Annotated Wizard of Oz* (1973). In 1956, Reilly & Lee, the publisher of the rest of the Oz series, issued its first edition of the first Oz book.

1956 Reilly & Lee Edition Illustrated by Dale Ulrey

The Wizard of Oz. Chicago: The Reilly & Lee Co., [1956]. 237 pages plus two unnumbered pages containing an Afterword by Edward Wagenknecht. Illustrated by Dale Ulrey. First edition in this form, three states:

1. *Textual points*: 32-page gatherings except for the final of 16 pages. The text illustrations are printed in black and red. Inserted endpapers: the front is a full-color map of Oz; the back is blank.

Cover: (Plate 16) light red-brown cloth, stamped on the front
in light brick-red and black, and on the spine in black. The
back cover is blank. Issued in a pictorial dust jacket (plate
17).

2. Similar to # 1 with the following exceptions: the book has
    been reimposed so that it has blank self-endpapers and a
    terminal gathering of 24 pages; it is bound in green cloth,
    stamped only on the spine in black. Copies of this state
    have been reported in a new dust jacket signed "Roycraft".

3. Similar to #s 1 and 2 with the following exceptions: the
    book has again been reimposed so that it is made up of 32-
    page gatherings except for one near the middle (the 5th
    gathering) of 24 pages; the text illustrations are printed in
    black and a second color, in the following order: blue,
    yellow, red, green, yellow, blue, red. Copies of this state
    have been reported in a new dust jacket by Dick Martin.

In 1964, Reilly & Lee replaced the Ulrey illustrations
with re-workings of some of the Denslow illustrations,
including a few from Denslow's other Oz-related publications,
as well as one (p. 53) that was later discovered to be wrongly
attributed to Denslow. The first printing in this form is bound
in imprinted cloth with a blue background, based on a 1900
poster for the Geo. M. Hill edition. In 1965, in order to make
the book uniform with the "white-cover" printings of the other
Baum Oz books (see below, pp. 138-139), it was reissued in
imprinted cloth with a white background showing on the front
Dorothy, the Scarecrow, and the Tin Woodman with a large
poppy in the background.

For details on other United States editions of the first Oz
book, see "The Oz Bookshelf" in *The Baum Bugle*, beginning
in the Spring 1965 issue.

British Printings

The following significant versions published in London
before the book reached public domain are known:

The New Wizard of Oz. London: Hodder & Stoughton, [copyright 1903, published 1906]. 261 pages. The contents are identical with the Bobbs-Merrill second edition, second state, except that the British publisher's name has been added on the title page beneath the American one; the verso has the three-entry copyright notice. The book is bound in light-green cloth, stamped in black, dark peach, and dark green, with the Hodder & Stoughton imprint on the spine. The cover illustrations are the same as those on the American version.

The Wizard of Oz. London: Hutchinson & Co., n.d. [1926]. 190 pages. This edition has no color plates, but many of Denslow's black-and-white illustrations are included. There are two states of the cover: the first is very dark brick-red cloth, stamped in black, with a paper label on the front with the same design as that for the fourth and fifth United States editions; the later state lacks the paper label. The size of leaf is smaller than United States printings: approximately 6 5/8 by 4 7/8 inches.

Wizard of Oz Story Book. London: Hutchinson & Co., n.d. [1940]. 64 pages. This edition, which does not mention L. Frank Baum, has reset type and a few of Denslow's textual illustrations. It is bound in pictorial wrappers with a still from the MGM movie on the front and back. Size of leaf is approximately 11 by 8 3/8 inches.

The Wizard of Oz. London. Hutchinson & Co., n.d. [ca. 1940]. 208 pages. This printing has reset type and replaces the Denslow color plates with 4 color stills and 4 color publicity photographs from the MGM movie. There are two states of the cover: pictorial paper-covered boards (plate 18), and light-green cloth stamped in black. No priority is known.

The Wizard of Oz. London: Hutchinson & Co., n.d. [1940]. 96 pages. This abridgment, bound in pictorial paper-covered boards (plate 19), contains 4 full-page black-and-white illustrations and a frontispiece in black and yellow by Denslow.

The Wizard of Oz. London: Hutchinson's Books for
Young People, [1947]. 171 pages. This edition contains 5
color plates by H.M. Brock as well as textual illustrations by
Denslow. Bound in pictorial paper-covered boards with a red
cloth spine (plate 20).

II. THE MARVELOUS LAND OF OZ

The Marvelous Land of Oz is almost as bibliographically
complex as *The Wonderful Wizard of Oz*. It was printed
with modifications several times from the original plates
during its first two years. Several variant binding cases were
used, and by 1906 the cover title had been shortened to *The
Land of Oz*. It is not unusual to find variant copies of the
book that combine components in something other than the
sequence in which they were created. Commonly observed
variants are described below in logical sequence.

The Marvelous Land of Oz. Chicago: The Reilly & Britton
Co., 1904. 287 pages. Illustrated by John R. Neill. First
edition, six states:

1. *Textual points*: Hand-lettered title page, beginning "The
   Marvelous | Land of Oz"; the date "1904" appears at
   the bottom of the page. (This date remained unchanged in
   subsequent printings as late as 1912.) The copyright
   notice on the verso of the title page has no publication date
   below it. The illustration on page [4] is quite large: the box
   containing the dedication is 6 1/4 inches tall. Two full-
   page text illustrations are misplaced: page [22] has
   Mombi threatening to turn Tip into a marble statue and
   page [27] has Mombi putting Jack in the stable. Two
   chapter tailpieces are misplaced: page 82 has a picture of
   Tip and page 158 has a picture of Jinjur. The inserted
   pictorial endpapers are printed in dark green on a thin,
   light-green stock. (In some copies the endpaper stock has
   faded to a tan or buff color.)

Color plates: 16 full-color inserts, tipped in facing the title page and pages 10, 56, 68, 78, 116, 142, 162, 174, 182, 204, 220, 242, 254, 260, 284. The color plates have typeset captions.

Cover: (Plate 21) various cover casings:

A) Light-green or red cloth stamped in navy blue, silver and green. (The navy blue is so dark that it often appears to be black.) The front cover and the spine carry the full title, *The Marvelous Land of Oz*, stamped only in blue. Immediately below the title on the front cover is "by L. Frank Baum". The spine has a horizontal rule at the top and a double rule at the bottom in blue, and a picture of Jinjur in blue and green. The publisher's imprint on the spine reads: "THE REILLY & BRITTON CO." The back cover has a picture of Jack Pumpkinhead in blue.

B) Red cloth with stamping identical with A except that the letters in "Marvelous Land of Oz" on the front cover are embellished with silver outlines.

C) Rose cloth with stamping identical with B including the silver embellishments.

The red and green forms of binding case A seem to have been issued simultaneously; two significant presentation copies, one in red and one in green, were inscribed by the author "July, 1904". Case A is normally found with the spine rules described above, but a few copies of both colors have been reported with no rules. Binding case B replaced the red form of A before first state text sheets were exhausted, and it is the binding most frequently seen on second state sheets. The green form of A is also occasionally found on second state sheets. Binding case C, which is a much lighter red than B, seems to have been the final form used before the cover title was shortened.

Dust jacket: A monochrome version of the binding design in dark green on very light-green stock. The front and back flaps are blank.

Size of leaf: 9 by 6 3/4 inches. *Thickness of volume:* 1 1/8 inches.

2. *Textual points:* The line "Published, July, 1904" has been added below the copyright notice on the verso of the title page. The illustration on page [4] is considerably reduced: the box is 5 3/8 inches tall. The illustrations on page [22] and page [27] are transposed. The tailpieces on pages 82 and 158 are also transposed.

Color plates: Same as #1.

Cover: State 2 appears most commonly in binding cases B and C, but copies in the light-green form of A occur with enough frequency to indicate that this form of binding case was still in stock when state 2 sheets were printed.

Shortened Cover Title

3. *Title page, textual points,* and *color plates:* Same as #2.

Cover: (Plate 22) red cloth. The stamping is similar to #2 with the following changes. The title on the front cover and on the spine has been shortened to *The Land of Oz.* On the front cover, the title is in silver letters outlined in navy blue. Below it has been added in navy blue "A Sequel to | The Wizard of Oz". The author's name has been shifted to the lower-right corner of the front cover. A single-rule border surrounds the stamping on the front cover. There are single rules at the top and bottom of the spine, and silver embellishments have been added to the picture of Jinjur. The publisher's imprint on the spine reads: "THE REILLY & | BRITTON CO." Several copies have been seen stamped in black rather than navy blue and printed on a thinner paper stock; they measure slightly less than 1 inch rather than 1 1/8 inches of ordinary copies.

4. *Title page, textual points,* and *color plates:* Same as #s 2 and 3 except that the text is printed on a heavy rough-surfaced stock, making a much bulkier book, about 1 3/8 inches thick including the covers. The endpapers are printed in green on a heavy, coated, cream-colored stock; some copies have been seen with the endpapers in dark green on a pea-green stock.

Cover: Same as #3 except that the stamping is usually in black, silver, and green; less frequently in navy blue, silver and green. Some copies (probably later) have been seen with a blank back cover.

A British issue was received at the British Museum on September 7, 1904. It contains the sheets of American state #1 in binding case B (including the American imprint on the spine). The title page is a cancel with imprint of "LONDON ⏐ Fleming H. Revell Company ⏐ 1904". This issue was produced to protect British copyright, and thus it is unlikely that any copies were intended for sale. A British issue which was probably released for sale was published in 1906 by Hodder & Stoughton of London. It contains the American state #2 sheets. The title page has been entirely relettered with a slight change in the spelling of the title: *The Marvellous Land of Oz.* The cover (plate 23) is similar to American state #3, but instead of "A Sequel to ⏐ The Wizard of Oz" it reads "By the author of ⏐ The Wizard of Oz". The cover is rose cloth, stamped in dark yellow, black, gray, white, and brown with the Hodder & Stoughton imprint on the spine.

Shortened Title-page Title

5. *Textual points, color plates,* and *cover:* The title on the title page has been shortened to *The Land of Oz.* A list of books below the author's name on the title page includes *Tik-Tok of Oz,* indicating that this state was printed about 1914. There is no date at the foot of the title page. The

page is not hand-lettered but has been set in type. Verso: same as #s 2, 3, and 4 above. Otherwise the state is the same as #4 above, with the blank back cover. One copy has been reported bound in orange, rather than red cloth, and several copies have been reported as being somewhat thinner and having only 12 color plates.

6. Same as #5 with the following exceptions: the number of the color plates has been reduced to 12, and the captions have been dropped; the endpapers are printed in medium green on white stock; the binding is off-white (or light-tan) cloth. This variant was printed about 1917. It is about 1 1/4 inch thick.

Subsequent printings carry the Reilly & Lee imprint. The earliest is similar to the sixth state, described above, except that the endpapers are printed in black and white and that the cover is stamped only in black and silver. Later printings are bound in various colors of cloth and have a pictorial paper label in colors on the front cover, similar to the stamped design of the third state of the first edition (plate 24). The silver and green embellishments have been removed from the spine. Some copies have black-and-white pictorial endpapers; in others the endpapers are blank. Also in some copies new captions have been added to the color plates. Although the regular version with 12 color plates seems to have continued in print, in 1925 a "Popular Edition" (plate 25) was issued with a single color plate (a frontispiece).* Around 1935, the use of color plates was discontinued.

In 1939, another "Popular Edition" was published, bound in paper-covered boards, and with a new cover design (plate 26). This is an oversize volume. Size of leaf: 9 7/16 by 7 inches. Beginning about the middle 1940s, another new cover design (plate 27) began to be used. Shortly thereafter, a new edition appeared, with text and running-titles entirely reset, and the copyright dates in Roman numerals ("MCMIV-MCMXXXII"). In 1965, the book appeared in the uniform

---

*The words "Popular Edition" appear in various locations and typestyles on the paper label. One copy, probably a binder's error, has been seen with 12 color plates but with "Popular Edition" on the paper label.

"white-cover" printings with a redrawing of the Neill cover design and the original typesetting.

In 1961, Dover Publications issued a paperbound photo-facsimile of the first edition, second state, in somewhat reduced size with the 16 color plates. In 1985, Books of Wonder, William Morrow published an edition containing all the color plates and textual illustrations and with the original pagination, but with reset type and without the pictorial endpapers.

III. OZMA OF OZ

Ozma of Oz. Chicago: The Reilly & Britton Co., [1907]. 270 pages. Illustrated by John R. Neill. First edition, five states:

1. *Textual points*: The publisher's advertisements facing the half-title page and at the end of the book offer two titles: *The Land of Oz* and *John Dough and the Cherub*. Fifth line of the "Author's Note", page [11]: some copies have the "O" present in "Ozma"; others do not. (Of the two significant presentation copies examined, only one has the "O". This suggests that the drop-out occurred during the first press run.) There are no inserted color plates; color is used in many of the text illustrations. The illustration on page [221] is in color. In some copies pages 135-[136], [153]-154, and [221]-222 are integral; in others, one, two, or all three leaves are cancels. Apparently the coloring on these pages suffered smudging or "offset" during printing and stacking of the sheets, and the worst of them were excised and replaced after the books were assembled. Inserted pictorial endpapers in color.

   Cover: (Plate 28) light-tan cloth, stamped in black, red, blue, and yellow. The publisher's name at the foot of the spine reads: "THE REILLY & | BRITTON CO." in large and small capital letters. The spine has a drawing of Ozma stamped in black, red, and yellow. The back cover shows the lion, the tiger, and the hen, peering over or through an "OZ" monogram.

SECONDARY BINDING: Before the stock of original sheets was exhausted a secondary binding case began to be used. It is identical with the cover described above except that the spine imprint reads: "Reilly & | Britton". One copy has been seen with blank endpapers.

Dust jacket: (Plate 29) Issued in a full-color dust jacket with an illustration on the front which is different from that on the binding. The back of the jacket and the front and rear flaps are blank.

Size of leaf: 9 by 6 3/4 inches. *Thickness of volume*: 7/8 inch.

A publisher's or salesman's dummy of *Ozma of Oz* is known. It contains only the first 32 pages of the book, sewn in 8-page gatherings. No text appears on the dedication page or the "List of Chapters" pages. Page [11] has the "O" present in "Ozma". The binding case is identical with that of the first state, except that the spine is blank. The volume measures a scant 1/2 inch thick.

Ozma of Oz was published in Canada by the Copp, Clark Co., Limited, of Toronto. The single known copy is identical with American first state copies (with the "O" present in "Ozma", page [11], pages 135-[136], [153]-154, and [221]-222 integral, and page [221] in color), but with a cancel title page with the Canadian imprint; the verso is blank. There is no publisher's imprint on the spine.

Later Printings

2. *Textual points*: Same as #1 with the following exceptions: the publisher's advertisement at the end of the book lists titles through *The Emerald City of Oz* (1910),* the "O" in "Ozma" on page [11] is missing; the illustration on page [221] is in black and white. All pages are integral.

*Since this advertisement has decorations drawn for Baum's *The Sea Fairies* (1911), this state appeared no earlier than 1911.

Some copies have pictorial and others have blank end-papers. The book is printed on a heavier weight paper and is about 1 1/4 inches thick including covers.

Cover: Same as the secondary binding case described above.

3. *Textual points*: Same as #2 except that the advertisement lists titles through *The Patchwork Girl of Oz* (1913). Blank endpapers.

Cover: Same as #2.

4. *Textual points*: Same as #s 2 and 3 except that the advertisement lists titles through *The Lost Princess of Oz* (1917), and the book measures about 1 1/16 inches thick including covers. Blank endpapers.

Cover: Same as #s 2 and 3 except that the back cover is blank. (One copy has been reported that retains the back cover illustration.)

5. *Textual points*: Same as #3 and 4 except that the advertisement lists titles through *The Tin Woodman of Oz* (1918).

Cover: Tan cloth, with pictorial paper label in colors on the front cover. (This label design appeared on the dust jackets of the previous states.) The spine is stamped in black only; at the foot is the imprint: "Reilly │ & Lee".

NOTE: The firm name "Reilly & Britton" did not become "Reilly & Lee" until 1919. Therefore it is possible that #5 sheets also exist in Reilly & Britton binding cases.

Subsequent printings of *Ozma of Oz* have the Reilly & Lee imprint on the title page. Copies have been noted with advertisements listing titles through *Glinda of Oz* (1920), through *Kabumpo in Oz* (1922), and through *The Cowardly Lion of Oz* (1923). Later printings have no advertisements. Some of the 1922 and 1923 copies and all later ones have the

"O" in "Ozma" on page [11] restored in a slightly different type face.

In 1929, a new cover label and jacket design (plate 30) by John R. Neill replaced the old one; it was used on all subsequent editions of *Ozma of Oz* until 1959. In 1931, a "Popular Edition" (plate 31) was issued which dispensed with the use of color within the book. Both the regular edition with color illustrations and the "Popular Edition" were issued simultaneously for several years. Around 1935 or a little earlier, the regular edition was discontinued and the "Popular Edition" was no longer so designated on its cover label. In all printings since then, the illustrations have been only in black and white.

In 1985, Dover Publications issued a paperbound photofacsimile of an early printing of *Ozma of Oz*, in somewhat reduced size and with the endpapers and illustrations in black and white.

IV. DOROTHY AND THE WIZARD IN OZ

Dorothy and the Wizard in Oz. Chicago: The Reilly & Britton Co., [1908]. 256 pages. Illustrated by John R. Neill. First edition, three major states:

1. *Textual points*: The publisher's advertisement on the verso of the half-title page lists three books: *The Land of Oz, Ozma of Oz,* and *John Dough and the Cherub*. The ownership page shows a picture of Dorothy and the final illustration in the book (page [257]) is a drawing of Ozma, with the words "The End". The book is made up of 16-page gatherings except for the last which contains 20 pages. Inserted pictorial endpapers in black and yellow.

Color plates: 16 full-color inserts, tipped in facing the title page and pages 16, 34, 50, 60, 80, 100, 122, 138, 146, 164, 192, 210, 220, 244, 252. Captions in black. (The color plates are figured into the pagination of the book.)

Cover: (Plate 32) light-blue cloth. On the front is a pictorial paper label in colors; the figures and the lettering are set against a metallic-gold background. The spine is lettered in black with a picture of the Tin Woodman in black and silver. The publisher's name appears at the foot: "THE REILLY & ꞁ BRITTON CO." in large and small capital letters.

SECONDARY BINDING: Before the original sheets were exhausted, a new binding case was used with a shorter spine imprint: "Reilly & ꞁ Britton".

Dust jacket: Issued in a full-color dust jacket with an illustration on the front which reproduces the label design. The back panel reproduces the publisher's advertisement on the verso of the half-title page. The front and rear flaps are blank.

Size of leaf: 9 by 6 3/4 inches. *Thickness of volume*: 1 inch.

Reilly & Britton also produced a Canadian issue which was published probably simultaneously with the first American state. This variant has the imprint of the Copp, Clark Co., Limited, of Toronto on the title page and horizontal rules at the foot of the spine rather than the publisher's name; copies have been seen ꞏ ith double or with triple spine rules.

Later Printings

2. Although there were several printings of *Dorothy and the Wizard in Oz* between 1908 and 1916, no major resetting of the text has been observed. About 1911, the publisher reprinted the book with a new advertisement listing Baum titles through *The Emerald City of Oz*. This state is on thicker paper, measuring between 1 1/4 and 1 3/8 inches thick including covers. The color plates of earlier copies of this state have captions in black; later copies have color plates without captions. The covers of earlier copies of #2 are essentially identical with the secondary binding described above; later copies have the spine stamped only in black; still later copies have a yellow rather than a gold background on

the front cover's pictorial label, and the spine imprint has been reset in capitals: "REILLY & | BRITTON".

Because several changes were made in the cover and color plates, a number of variant copies of #2 were created. Apparently the changes in individual components were made before existing supplies were exhausted. The following combinations have been observed and are listed here in logical order:

A) Same as the first state except that the book contains an advertisement listing titles through *The Emerald City of Oz*. The spine imprints reads: "Reilly & | Britton".

B) Same as variant A except that the plates have no captions and the spine is stamped only in black.

C) Same as variant B except that the pictorial paper label on the front cover has a yellow background rather than gold and the spine imprint has been reset: "REILLY & | BRITTON". This variant appeared about 1915.

Re-imposed Form of the Text

3. About 1916, presumably to cut production costs, Reilly & Britton published a re-imposed version of *Dorothy and the Wizard in Oz*. By deleting two leaves and re-imposing the printing plates, the format of the book was adjusted so that the final gathering required only 16 pages rather than the irregular 20 pages of earlier printings. The deletions were the half-title, the publisher's advertisement that appeared on the verso of the half-title, and the picture of Ozma at the end of the book. At the same time the ownership-page drawing first used in *Rinkitink in Oz* (1916), showing a group of children reading a book, was substituted for the original one. The book still contains the 16 color plates, without captions. All copies seen of the re-imposed book have black-and-white endpapers, and the pictorial label on the front cover is printed with a yellow background rather than metallic gold; the spine imprint has again been reset: "Reilly & | Britton". A late

form of this state is known which is in every way identical, including the Reilly & Britton title page, except that the spine imprint reads: "Reilly ⏐ & Lee". Copies have been seen in very light blue and light blue-green cloth.

Subsequent printings of *Dorothy and the Wizard in Oz* carry the Reilly & Lee imprint on the title page. Copies have been seen with advertisements listing titles through *The Magic of Oz* (1919), *Glinda of Oz* (1920), and *The Hungry Tiger of Oz* (1926); others have no advertisements. Some of the 1920 copies and all subsequent color-plate printings have new, reset captions in blue on the color plates.

In 1930, a "Popular Edition" appeared with only one color plate, a frontispiece. The picture of Dorothy was deleted from the cover label to make room for the words "Popular Edition" (plate 33). As the color plates were included in the pagination of previous printings, the pages had to be renumbered. For some reason, the first half of the book was not repaginated, and the gaps were filled by tipping in six black-and-white illustrations from *The Lost King of Oz* (1925) and *The Gnome King of Oz* (1927); the second half of the book v as repaginated. This curious hybrid also occurs in some copies of the regular edition, with 12 of the original color plates. (One copy has been reported with 2 color plates and only 5 black-and-white inserts.)

Shortly after 1930, the book was entirely and correctly repaginated and the inappropriate black-and-white inserts were dropped in subsequent states of the "Popular Edition" and the regular edition. The contents page in these states was not reset, and consequently the page references are incorrect. Sometime between 1930 and 1935, the color plates and the pictorial endpapers were discontinued entirely, and the cover label omits both the words "Popular Edition" and the picture of Dorothy. About 1938, an edition in smaller format (size of leaf: 8 3/16 by 6 1/8 inches) appeared, printed on cheaper paper stock and with 12-page gatherings. The book contains a new cover label (plate 34) and a corrected contents page. Reilly & Lee prepared this form of the book for sale by Sears,

Roebuck and Company. About 1947, *Dorothy and the Wizard in Oz* was given a new cover label (plate 35) drawn by the anonymous artist who drew the new cover label for *The Land of Oz*. In 1964, the book appeared in the uniform "white-cover" printings with a redrawing of the original 1908 cover design, including the picture of Dorothy.

The only recent printing with color illustrations was published in Toronto by Coles Publishing Company, Limited, 1980. It is somewhat larger than the original edition (approximately 11 by 8 1/2 inches).

In 1984, Dover Publications issued a paperbound photofacsimile of the first edition of *Dorothy and the Wizard in Oz*, in black-and-white. The original ownership page and pictorial endpapers are omitted.

V. THE ROAD TO OZ

As with other Oz books already described, first-state copies of the text sheets of *The Road to Oz* have been found in later binding cases. The description here indicates the usual arrangement of the color-tinted text sheets. Several copies, however, have been discovered that have different arrangements of the colors. They are described in a note following the main description.* Alterations in the colors of the gatherings do not necessarily imply a separate press run. A printer might easily have placed, for example, a stack of green sheets on the press while there remained some blue sheets still being run through the machine.

The Road to Oz. Chicago: The Reilly & Britton Co., [1909]. 261 pages. Illustrated by John R. Neill. First edition, four major states:

1. *Textual points*: There are two pages of advertisements at the end of the book: page [263] lists Baum books published under the pseudonym "Laura Bancroft," and

---

*Collectors and scholars should take special care in describing the tinted pages, as the colors seem to have been particularly subject to fading.

page [264] lists four other Baum titles: *The Land of Oz,*
Ozma of Oz, Dorothy and the Wizard of [sic] *Oz,* and
John Dough and the Cherub. There are no color plates.
The gatherings are printed on variously tinted stock: off-
white (pages [1]-32), lavender (33-64), gray (65-96),
light blue (97-128), salmon (129-160), tan (161-192),
light green (193-256), tan (257-[264]). The first copies
off the press have perfect type in the words "Toto on",
page 34, line 4, and in the numeral "121" on page 121;
and the numeral and caption are present beneath the
illustration on page 129. Later copies may show type
damage on either or both pages 34 and 121, and in still
later copies the caption and numeral are dropped from
page 129. Inserted pictorial endpapers printed in black
and red on tan stock of the same quality as the text stock.

Cover: (Plate 36) light-green, smooth fine-grained cloth,
stamped in black, dark green, tan, and red. (Some copies
have been reported in a coarse-weave cloth sometimes
described as buckram.) The back cover has silhouette
portraits of Dorothy and Ozma within a sunburst effect.
The spine is stamped in black, dark green, and red, with an
illustration of Toto in dark green. The publisher's name at
the foot of the spine reads: "Reilly & ⎢ Britton".

SECONDARY BINDING: Some copies have the spine imprint
reset in large and small captials: "REILLY & ⎢ BRITTON".

Dust jacket: (Plate 37) issued in a full-color dust jacket. The
front panel has an illustration that differs from the front
cover design, printed in full-color with a metallic gold background. The back panel reproduces the advertisement that
appears on page [264]. The front and rear flaps are blank.

Size of leaf: 9 by 6 5/8 inches. *Thickness of volume*: 1 1/16
inches.

NOTE: Because there is insufficient physical evidence to
classify as separate printings minor variations among
copies of *The Road to Oz* printed on color-tinted stock,

we have grouped all such copies as part of state 1. We offer below descriptions of a number of variant copies that differ from the normal arrangement of color-tinted text sheets. The variants are listed roughly in the sequence of progressive type damage. The reader should remember that so long as the book was in continuous production and was assembled in the bindery as orders came from the publisher to bind up a new group of copies, it was always possible for sheets of different vintages to be assembled to produce mixed copies.

A) Apparently part of the earliest copies of state 1, but it differs in having pages 33-64 on off-white rather than lavender stock. Earlier binding case.

B) Apparently part of the earliest copies of state 1, but it differs in having pages 113-128 on light green rather than light-blue stock. Secondary binding case.

C) The same as later copies of state 1, with plate wear at all the places noted. It differs in having the terminal gathering printed on salmon stock rather than tan. Earlier binding case.

D) The same as later copies of state 1, with plate wear at all the places noted. It differs in having the tinted text sheets arranged in the following pattern: off-white (pages [1]-16), gray (17-32), lavender (33-64), gray (65-96), light blue (97-128), salmon (129-160), tan (161-192), salmon (193-208), light green (209-256), tan (257-[264]). The endpapers are of highly calendered stock. Secondary binding case.

E) The same as later copies of state 1, with plate wear at all places noted, except that page 34, line 4 has "Toto on" in perfect type. (It has been suggested that the type has been reset at that place; it is unbroken in later printings.) As with variant C, it has the terminal gathering printed on salmon stock rather than tan. Earlier binding case.

F) The same as later copies of state 1, with plate wear at all places noted, except that page 34, line 4 has "Toto on" in perfect type. It differs in having the terminal gathering printed on gray stock rather than tan. Secondary binding case.

Later Printings

2. *Textual points*: Same as variants E and F described above (with "Toto on", page 34, in perfect type) except that there is a publisher's advertisement on the verso of the ownership page listing Oz titles through *Rinkitink in Oz* (1916); there are no advertisements at the end of the book. The entire book is printed on white stock and the endpapers are blank.

Cover: Similar to the earlier covers except that the back cover is blank. The publisher's name on the spine reads: "Reilly & ǀ Britton".

3. *Textual points*: Same as #2 except that the advertisement lists titles through *The Lost Princess of Oz* (1917).

Cover: Same as #2.

4. *Textual points*: Same as #s 2 and 3 except that the advertisement lists titles through *The Tin Woodman of Oz* (1918). The book is printed on bulkier stock so that with the cover the volume measures about 1 1/4 inches thick.

Cover: Same as #s 2 and 3 except that the design is stamped on off-white (or light-tan) cloth.

SECONDARY BINDINGS: Copies of #4 sheets, including the Reilly & Britton title page, have been seen in gray-green cloth with the spine imprint reading "Reilly ǀ & Lee". One copy of this variant has been noted in bright emerald-green cloth.

One green-bound copy has been reported without any advertisements. The back cover is blank, and the spine imprint reads: "Reilly & | Britton". When this book was printed is not known. That it does not have advertisements argues for a date of between 1910-1915, but its thickness (1 1/2 inches) may indicate that it was published at a later date.

Subsequent printings of *The Road to Oz* carry the Reilly & Lee imprint on the title page and have pictorial paper labels on the front cover. This label design is identical with the front panel of the original dust jacket except that the background of the design is printed in blue or, later, in yellow rather than metallic gold. Copies have been seen with advertisements listing titles through *The Magic of Oz* (1919), *Glinda of Oz* (1920), and *The Hungry Tiger of Oz* (1926). Other copies, probably later, have no publisher's advertisements.

In 1986, Dover Publications issued a paperbound photo-facsimile of an early printing of *The Road to Oz*, in somewhat reduced size, printed on white stock with the pictorial endpapers reproduced in black-and-white.

VI. THE EMERALD CITY OF OZ

The Emerald City of Oz. Chicago: The Reilly & Britton Co., [1910]. 296 pages. Illustrated by John R. Neill. First edition, four states:

1. *Textual points*: The publisher's advertisement on the verso of the ownership page lists five titles: *The Road to Oz, The Land of Oz, Ozma of Oz, Dorothy and the Wizard in Oz,* and *John Dough and the Cherub.* Inserted pictorial endpapers in black and orange.

Color plates: 16 full-color inserts embellished with metallic-green ink, tipped in facing the title page and pages 24, 54, 74, 108, 116, 136, 166, 186, 222, 232, 240, 258, 264, 282, 292. There are no typeset captions on the plates, although some have hand-lettered captions within the drawings.

Cover: (Plate 38) light-blue or dark-blue cloth. (Although dark-blue copies are rarer, no priority has been established.)

On the front cover is a pictorial paper label showing a number of characters traveling through the city; the label is printed in colors and metallic green against a silver background. The spine is lettered in black with a picture of a rabbit in black and silver. The publisher's name appears at the foot of the spine: "Reilly & | Britton".

Dust jacket: Issued in a full-color dust jacket with an illustration on the front which reproduces the label design, including the metallic green. The back panel reproduces, in different type, the publisher's advertisement on the verso of the half-title page. The front and rear flaps are blank.

Size of leaf: 9 by 6 3/4 inches. *Thickness of volume*: 1 1/4 inches.

Several copies have been reported with the imprint of the Copp, Clark Co., Limited, of Toronto. Except for the imprint on the title page and spine, this issue is identical with the American first state; most copies are bound in dark-blue cloth, but one copy has been reported in light-blue.

Later Printings

2. *Textual points*: Same as #1 except that the book is printed on heavier paper stock, resulting in a volume about 1 3/8 inches thick.

Color plates: Same as #1 except that in most copies the metallic-green ink is a duller shade.

Cover: (Plate 39) bright-green cloth, with a pictorial paper label on the front derived from designs used for the endpapers of *Dorothy and the Wizard in Oz*. The spine stamping is identical with that of the earlier binding case.

NOTE: In the first edition of *Bibliographia Oziana* this variant was described as the first state text sheets in a secondary binding case. But the thickness of the volume and type degeneration (especially noticeable on the numerals for pages 96, 104, 232, and 286) provide evidence that copies in this binding are made up of a later printing rather than leftover sheets.

3. *Textual points*: Same as #s 1 and 2 except that the publisher's advertisement lists titles through *The Lost Princess of Oz* (1917).

Color plates: The number of color plates has been reduced to 12, and they lack the metallic-green embellishments.

Cover: Same as #2.

4. *Textual points*: Same as #s 1, 2, and 3 except that the advertisement lists titles through *The Tin Woodman of Oz* (1918), and the endpapers are in black and white.

Color plates: Same as #3.

Cover: Same as #s 2 and 3 except that there is no silver on the spine.

SECONDARY BINDING: Copies made up of #3 sheets, including the Reilly & Britton title page, have been seen in light-green cloth with the publisher's name on the spine: "Reilly | & Lee".

Subsequent printings of *The Emerald City of Oz* carry the Reilly & Lee imprint. Copies are known with publisher's advertisements through *The Tin Woodman of Oz* (1918), *Glinda of Oz* (1920), and *The Hungry Tiger of Oz* (1926); other copies presumably printed later have no advertisements. Copies printed in 1920 and later have typeset captions added to the color plates. In 1929, a third cover label and jacket design (plate 40), by John R. Neill, replaced the old one and appeared on all printings up to around 1960. About 1935, the color plates were discontinued.

VII. THE PATCHWORK GIRL OF OZ

The Patchwork Girl of Oz. Chicago: The Reilly & Britton Co., [1913]. 340 pages. Illustrated by John R. Neill. First edition:

Textual points: There are five pages of publisher's advertisements at the end of the book giving synopses of *The Land of Oz, Ozma of Oz, Dorothy and the Wizard in Oz, The Road to Oz,* and *The Emerald City of Oz.* Preceding these synopses is an announcement on page [343] reading "You Will Be Glad to Know . . . That There Are Five More Oz Books . . ." accompanied by half-tone photographs of the five book covers. The earliest copies of *The Patchwork Girl of Oz* have the words "CHAP. THREE" on page 35 positioned so that the "C" overlaps the text. This error was corrected, probably during the first printing, by moving the two words to the right. There are no inserted color plates; color is used in many of the text illustrations. Pictorial self-endpapers in color.

Cover: (Plate 41) light-green cloth, stamped in dark green, red, and yellow. A drawing of the Woozy in red and dark green appears on the spine. The publisher's imprint at the foot of the spine reads: "Reilly & | Britton"; the "R" in the imprint is 3/16 inch high, and the ampersand has a 1/16 inch opening at the top.

SECONDARY BINDING: Light-tan cloth, otherwise identical with the cover described above except that the spine imprint has been reset in very slightly different type: the "R" is 5/32 inch high and the opening at the top of the ampersand is 1/32 inch. See note below.

Dust jacket: (Plate 42) issued in a full-color dust jacket with a different illustration, on the front, back, and spine, from that which appears on the binding. The front and back flaps are blank.

NOTE: Until the publication of the first edition of *Bibliographia Oziana,* it was assumed that the light-tan binding case, which is scarcer than the light green, was earlier than or simultaneous with the light green. The following facts, however, lead to the conclusion that the light tan is a secondary binding. The different settings of the spine imprint indicate that the two binding cases were not

manufactured at the same time; it is significant that copies with the early placement of "CHAP. THREE" have been seen only in light-green cloth (copies with the later placement are known in both light green and light tan). In addition, at least two light-tan copies have been examined with the free halves of the *Patchwork Girl of Oz* endpapers excised and the paste-down halves present under the paste-downs of inserted endpapers for *The Land of Oz*. The new endpapers were apparently inserted during the binding process because of defects on the original endpapers. *The Land of Oz* endpapers are those associated with the sixth state of that book, which appeared ca. 1917.*
None of these indications is conclusive in itself, but taken together, they strongly suggest that the light-tan binding case is later than the light-green and dates from around 1917.

Size of leaf: 9 by 6 5/8 inches. Thickness of volume: 1 1/4 inches.

The Patchwork Girl of Oz is known in a Canadian issue with the imprint of the Copp, Clark Co., Limited, of Toronto on the title page and spine. It is bound in light-green cloth and has the later positioning of "CHAP. THREE".

Later Printings

Subsequent printings of *The Patchwork Girl of Oz* have the Reilly & Lee imprint and are bound in various colors of cloth stamped in black, yellow, and red. The earliest is almost identical with the Reilly & Britton edition in the

---

*While the first edition of *Bibliographia Oziana* was in press, another light-tan copy of *The Patchwork Girl of Oz* with *Land of Oz* endpapers was reported. It also indicates, though less obviously, that the light-tan binding case is secondary. The endpapers in this copy, which are in dark green on pea-green stock, are those associated with late copies (ca. 1913-14) of the fourth state of *The Marvelous Land of Oz*. That this *Patchwork Girl of Oz* has been altered in exactly the same way as the copies described above (an alteration found in no other early Oz book) suggests that both copies were cased around 1917. Hence the earlier *Marvelous Land of Oz* endpapers were probably leftovers in the bindery.

secondary binding, with the Woozy on the spine in red and dark green. Copies with advertisements on the verso of the half-title page through *The Magic of Oz* (1919) have the Woozy in black. Later copies with advertisements through *Kabumpo in Oz* (1922) and *The Cowardly Lion of Oz* (1923) and copies without advertisements on the verso of the half-title page (which are probably still later) have the Woozy in red and black. The announcement on page [343] is omitted in Reilly & Lee printings.

Copies printed after 1930 have pictorial paper labels on their front covers. This label design is identical with that which appeared as the front panel of dust jackets of the previous states. The picture of the Woozy on the spine has been replaced by one of Tik-Tok taken from the spine of *Tik-Tok of Oz*. By 1935, the color printing in the text was discontinued, leaving the endpapers and illustrations in black and white. The chapter numbers at the beginning of each chapter had been printed in color and were now also eliminated.

VIII. TIK-TOK OF OZ

Tik-Tok of Oz. Chicago: The Reilly & Britton Co., [1914]. 272 pages. Illustrated by John R. Neill. First edition, three states:

1. *Textual points*: The publisher's advertisement on the verso of the half-title page lists six Oz titles; the last is *The Patchwork Girl of Oz*. Inserted pictorial endpapers in full color. The front is a map of the Land of Oz and the back a map of the surrounding countries.*

   Color plates: 12 full-color inserts with no captions, tipped in facing the title page and pages 40, 72, 90, 108, 132, 142, 174, 196, 216, 230, 264.

*The map of Oz was reprinted in color in 1920 and given away with Oz books sold in that year. On the verso of the map is the flag of Oz. At an unknown time, probably early or middle 1920s, the maps were reprinted in black and white on a single sheet, with the map of Oz on one side and the map of surrounding countries on the other. In 1927, the map of Oz was again reprinted, this time with instructions on the same sheet for a coloring contest.

Cover: (Plate 43) medium-blue cloth. On the front is a pictorial paper label in colors. There are horizontal double rules at the top and bottom of the spine. The publisher's imprint on the spine reads: "Reilly & Britton".

Dust jacket: Issued in a full-color dust jacket with an identical illustration on the front and the back which reproduces the label design. The front flap has a blurb for the story. The back flap advertises *Little Wizard Stories of Oz* (1914).

Size of leaf: 9 by 6 3/4 inches. *Thickness of volume:* 1 1/4 inches.

An issue with the imprint of the Copp, Clark Co., Limited, of Toronto on the title page and spine is known. It is otherwise identical with the American first state.

Later Printings

2. *Textual points:* Same as #1 except that the publisher's advertisement lists titles through *The Lost Princess of Oz* (1917). Because it is printed on somewhat thinner stock, the book is 1 1/8 inches thick.

Color plates: Same as #1.

Cover: Same as #1 except that some copies have been seen without the double horizontal rules at the top and bottom of the spine.

3. *Textual points:* Same as #s 1 and 2 except that the publisher's advertisement lists titles through *The Tin Woodman of Oz* (1918) and the endpapers are printed only in green. The book is 1 1/4 inches thick.

Color plates: Same as #s 1 and 2 except for the location within the book and for the fact that most face to the rear.

Cover: Same as #s 1 and 2 except that the book is bound in dark-red cloth, with no horizontal rules on the spine.

SECONDARY BINDING: Copies made of #3 sheets, including the Reilly & Britton title page, have been seen bound in light-green cloth with the publisher's name printed on the spine: "Reilly | & Lee".

Subsequent printings of *Tik-Tok of Oz* containing color plates have the Reilly & Lee imprint on the title page and have blank endpapers. Copies have been reported with publisher's advertisements through *The Magic of Oz* (1919) and *Glinda of Oz* (1920). Later Reilly & Lee copies have no publisher's advertisements, and they add captions to the color plates. Around 1935, the color plates were discontinued.

IX. THE SCARECROW OF OZ

The Scarecrow of Oz. Chicago: The Reilly & Britton Co., [1915]. 288 pages. Illustrated by John R. Neill. First edition, three states:

1. *Textual points*: The publisher's advertisement on the verso of the half-title page lists eight Oz titles; the last is *The Scarecrow of Oz*. Inserted pictorial endpapers in black and white.

   Color plates: 12 full-color inserts with no captions, tipped in facing the title page and pages 16, 54, 84, 120, 136, 172, 200, 234, 248, 264, 280.

   Cover: (Plate 44) bright-green cloth. On the front is a pictorial paper label in colors. The publisher's name on the spine reads: "Reilly & | Britton". One copy has been reported with horizontal double rules at the top and bottom of the spine and bound in dark-green cloth. The paper label has an additional color; pink appears on the scarecrow's glove, face, and the rim of his hat, and on one of the crows' bonnets. Priority is unknown, though it is possible that this variant is an advance copy.

   Dust jacket: Issued in a full-color dust jacket with an identical illustration on the front and on the back which reproduces the label design. The front flap has a blurb for the story. The back flap advertises Chester H. Lawrence's *Santa Claus in Toyland* and Edith Mitchell's *The Otherside Book.*

Size of leaf: 9 by 6 5/8 inches. *Thickness of volume*: 1 7/16 inches.

An issue with the imprint of the Copp, Clark Co., Limited, of Toronto on the title page and spine is known. It is otherwise identical with the American first state in the standard binding.

Later Printings

2. *Textual points*: Same as #1 except that the publisher's advertisement lists titles through *The Lost Princess of Oz* (1917).

Color plates: Same as #1.

Cover: Same as #1 except that the book is bound in very dark green cloth. There are no horizontal rules on the spine.

3. *Textual points*: Same as #s 1 and 2 except that the publisher's advertisement lists titles through *The Tin Woodman of Oz* (1918).

Color plates and *cover*: Same as #2. Copies have been seen in dark-green and in light-blue cloth.

Subsequent printings of *The Scarecrow of Oz* carry the Reilly & Lee imprint. Copies have been seen with advertisements through *The Tin Woodman of Oz* (1918) and *Glinda of Oz* (1920), with no captions on the color plates. Another printing with advertisements through *The Cowardly Lion of Oz* (1923) adds captions to the color plates. Printings with no advertisements, which are probably later, also have captions on the color plates. Around 1935, the color plates were discontinued. For a brief period around 1935 the book was issued with just one of the color plates as a frontispiece. In 1940, an oversize "Popular Edition" was issued with a new cover design (plate 45). Size of leaf: 9 7/16 by 7 inches.

X. RINKITINK IN OZ

Rinkitink in Oz. Chicago: The Reilly & Britton Co., [1916]. 314 pages. Illustrated by John R. Neill. First edition, two states:

1. *Textual points*: There is no publisher's advertisement. Pictorial self-endpapers in black and white.

Color plates: 12 full-color inserts with no captions, tipped in facing the title page and pages 48, 104, 136, 152, 176, 208, 228, 264, 280, 296, 310.

Cover: (Plate 46) very light blue cloth. (One copy has been reported in light-green cloth.) On the front is a pictorial paper label in colors. The publisher's name on the spine reads: "Reilly &   Britton".

Dust jacket: Issued in a full-color dust jacket with an identical illustration on the front and the back which reproduces the label design. The front flap has a blurb for the story. The back flap advertises Myra G. Reed's *Jinks and Betty* and Norma Bright Carson's and Florence E. Bright's *Children's Own Story Book*.

Size of leaf: 9 by 6 5/8 inches. *Thickness of volume*: 1 1/2 inches.

Copies have been seen with the imprint of the Copp, Clark Co., Limited, of Toronto on the spine and title page. In all other respects they are identical with the first American state except that "Made in U.S.A." appears at the foot of the copyright page.

PLATE 1
(Page 26)

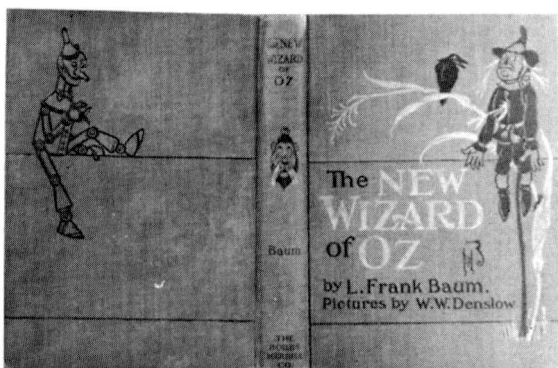

PLATE 2
(Page 29)

PLATE 3
(Page 30)

PLATE 4
(Page 34)

PLATE 5
(Page 35)

PLATE 6
(Page 35)

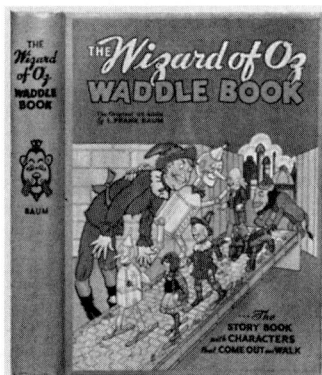

PLATE 7
(Page 36)

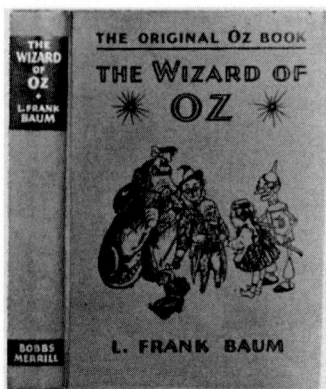

PLATE 8
(Page 37)

PLATE 9
(Page 37)

PLATE 10
(Page 37)

PLATE 11
(Page 38)

PLATE 12
(Page 39)

PLATE 13
(Page 39)

PLATE 14
(Page 41)

PLATE 15
(Page 41)

PLATE 16
(Page 43)

PLATE 17
(Page 43)

PLATE 18
(Page 44)

PLATE 19
(Page 44)

PLATE 20
(Page 45)

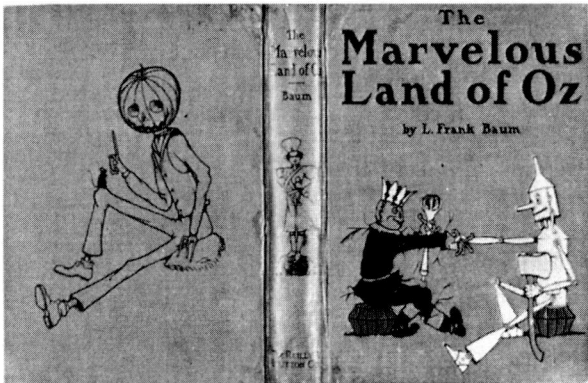

PLATE 21
(Page 46)

PLATE 22
(Page 47)

PLATE 23
(Page 48)

PLATE 24
(Page 49)

PLATE 25
(Page 49)

PLATE 26
(Page 49)

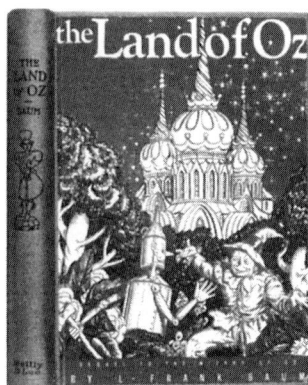

PLATE 27
(Page 49)

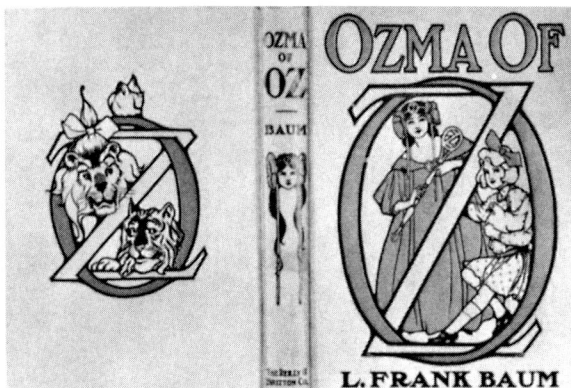

PLATE 28
(Page 50)

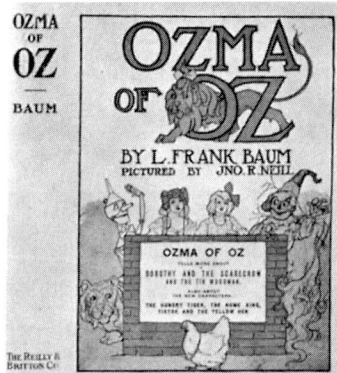

PLATE 29
(Page 51)

PLATE 30
(Page 53)

PLATE 31
(Page 53)

PLATE 32
(Page 53)

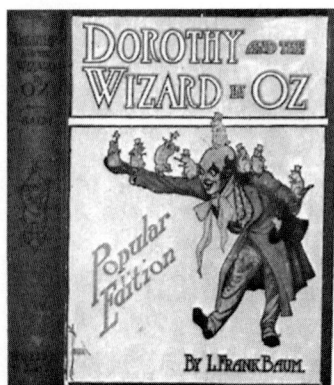

PLATE 33
(Page 56)

PLATE 34
(Page 56)

PLATE 35
(Page 57)

PLATE 36
(Page 58)

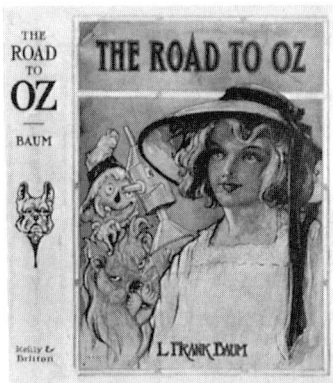

PLATE 37
(Page 58)

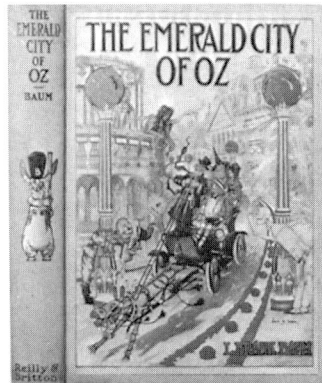

PLATE 38
(Page 61)

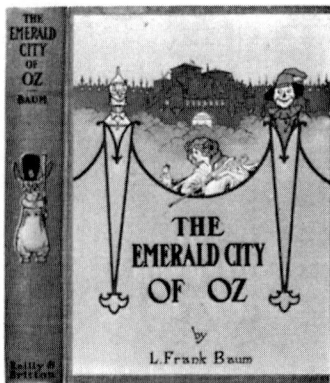

PLATE 39
(Page 62)

PLATE 40
(Page 63)

PLATE 41
(Page 64)

PLATE 42
(Page 64)

PLATE 43
(Page 67)

PLATE 44
(Page 68)

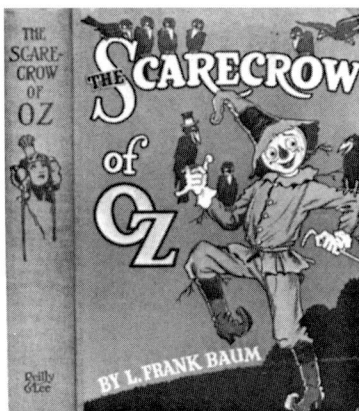

PLATE 45
(Page 70)

PLATE 46
(Page 70)

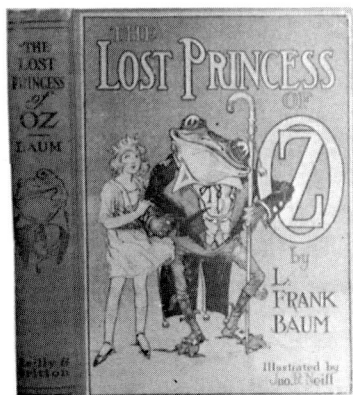

PLATE 47
(Page 72)

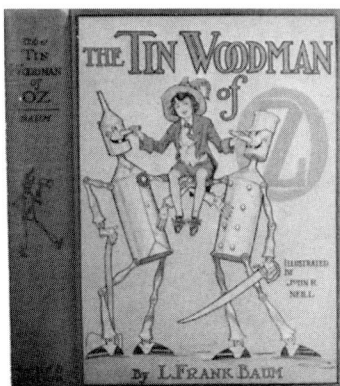

PLATE 48
(Page 73)

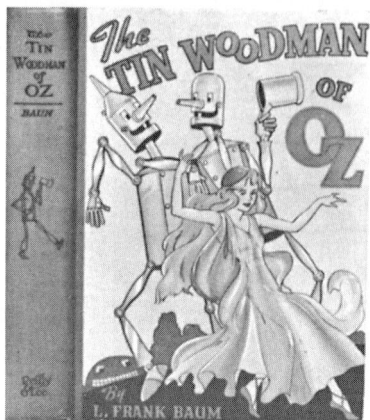

PLATE 49
(Page 74)

PLATE 50
(Page 74)

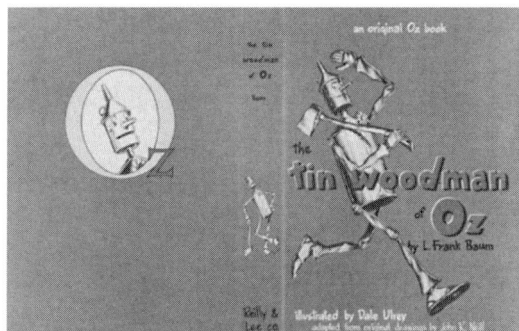

PLATE 51
(Page 74)

PLATE 52
(Page 74)

PLATE 53
(Page 76)

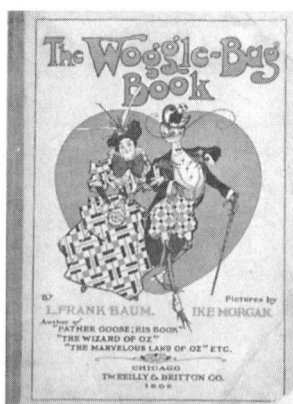

PLATE 54
(Page 79)

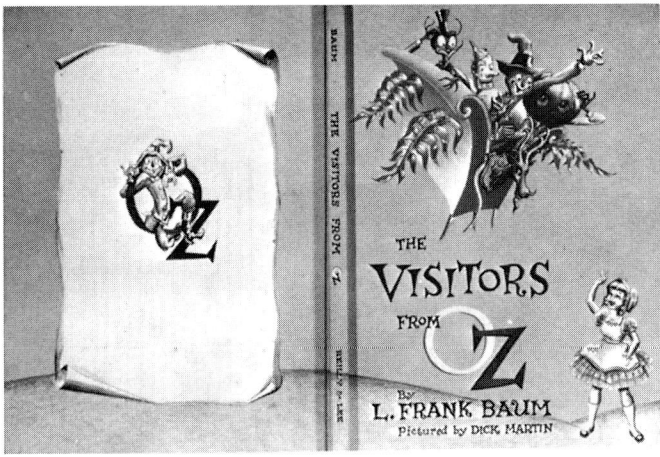

PLATE 55
(Page 81)

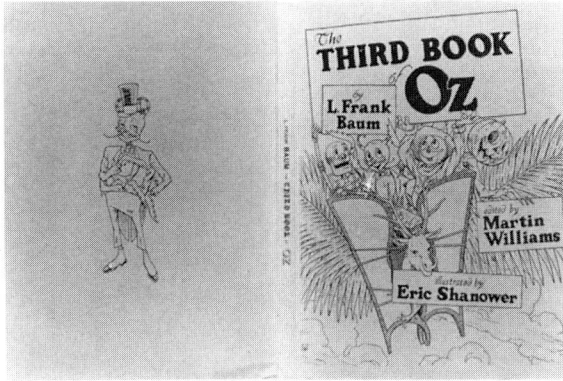

PLATE 56
(Page 82)

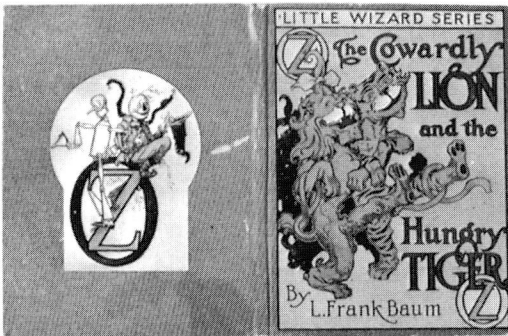

PLATE 57
(Page 83)

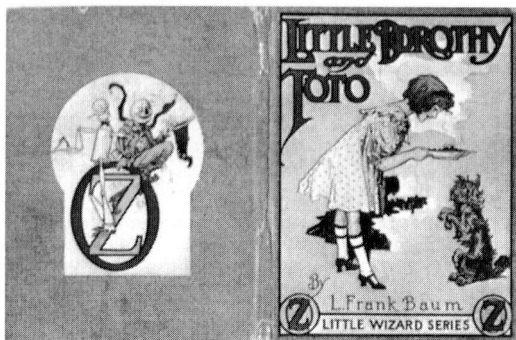

PLATE 58
(Page 83)

PLATE 59
(Page 83)

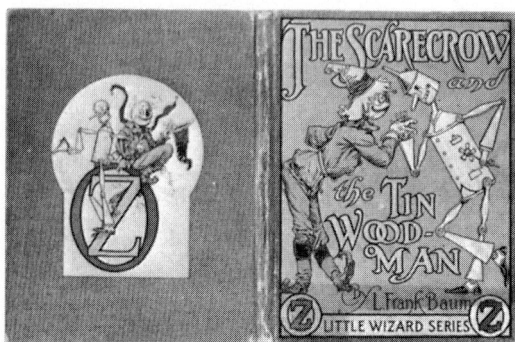

PLATE 60
(Page 83)

PLATE 61
(Page 83)

PLATE 62
(Page 83)

PLATE 63
(Page 83)

PLATE 64
(Page 83)

PLATE 65
(Page 84)

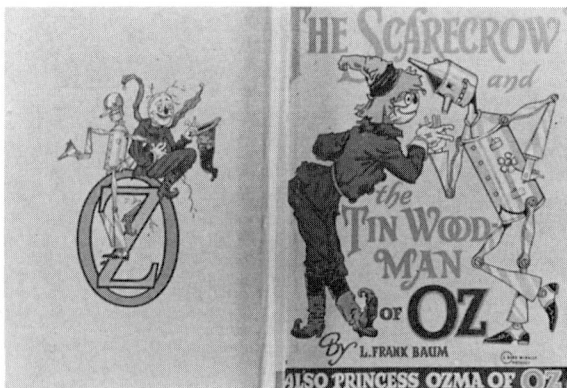

PLATE 66
(Page 85)

PLATE 67
(Page 85)

PLATE 68
(Page 85)

PLATE 69
(Page 86)

PLATE 70
(Page 88)

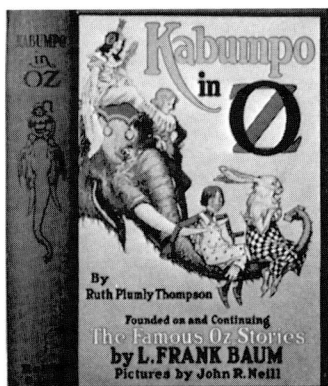

PLATE 71
(Page 89)

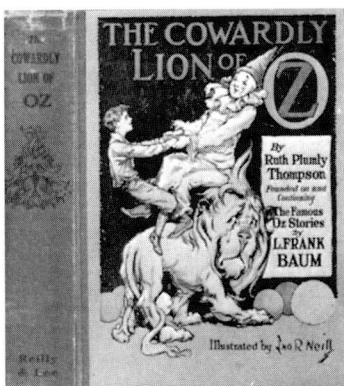

PLATE 72
(Page 90)

PLATE 73
(Page 91)

PLATE 74
(Page 92)

PLATE 75
(Page 93)

PLATE 76
(Page 94)

PLATE 77
(Page 95)

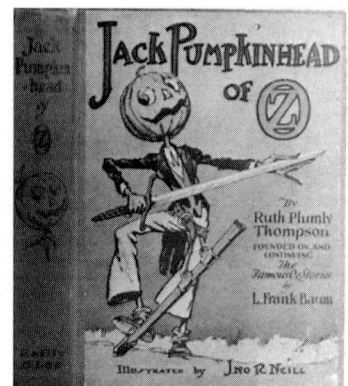

PLATE 78
(Page 96)

PLATE 79
(Page 97)

PLATE 80
(Page 97)

PLATE 81
(Page 98)

PLATE 82
(Page 99)

PLATE 83
(Page 100)

PLATE 84
(Page 101)

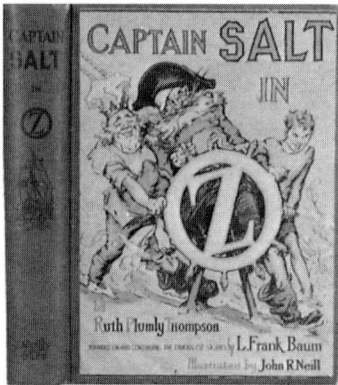

PLATE 85
(Page 101)

PLATE 86
(Page 102)

PLATE 87
(Page 103)

PLATE 88
(Page 104)

PLATE 89
(Page 105)

PLATE 90
(Page 106)

PLATE 91
(Page 107)

PLATE 92
(Page 107)

PLATE 93
(Page 107)

PLATE 94
(Page 108)

PLATE 95
(Page 109)

PLATE 96
(Page 109)

PLATE 97
(Page 110)

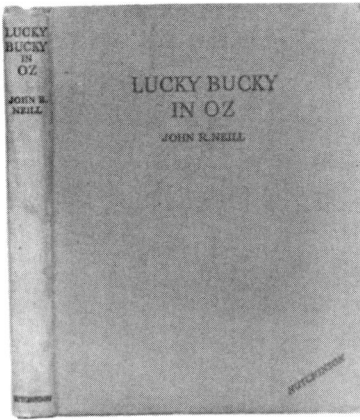

PLATE 98
(Page 111)

PLATE 99
(Page 112)

PLATE 100
(Page 114)

PLATE 101
(Page 115)

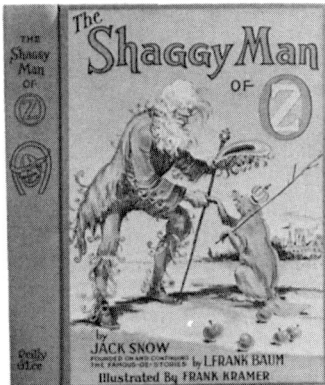

PLATE 102
(Page 115)

PLATE 103
(Page 117)

PLATE 104
(Page 117)

PLATE 105
(Page 118)

PLATE 106
(Page 119)

PLATE 107
(Page 121)

PLATE 108
(Page 122)

PLATE 109
(Page 123)

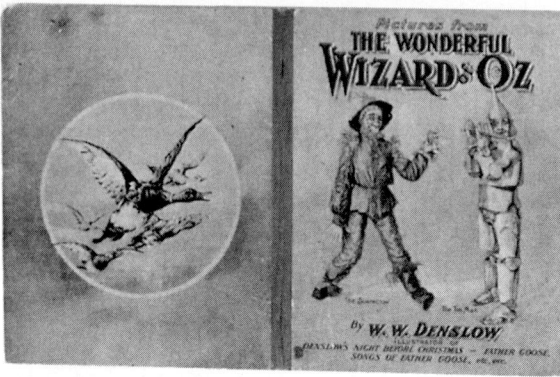

PLATE 110
(Page 125)

PLATE 111
(Page 125)

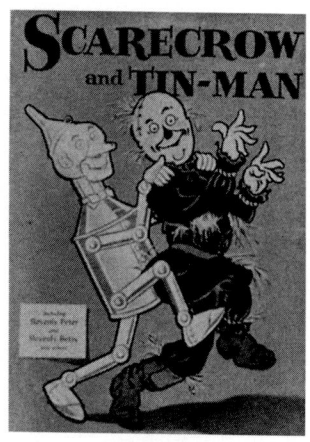

PLATE 112
(Page 126)

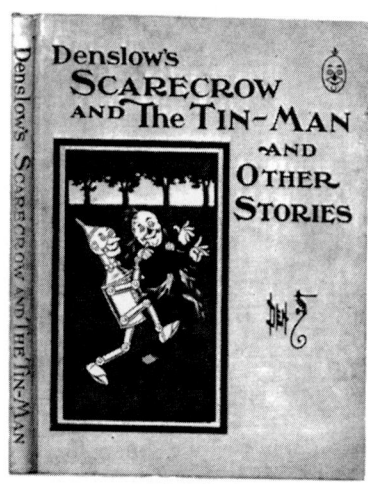

PLATE 113
(Page 127)

PLATE 114
(Page 129)

PLATE 115
(Page 131)

PLATE 116
(Page 132)

PLATE 117
(Page 133)

PLATE 118
(Page 133)

PLATE 119
(Page 133)

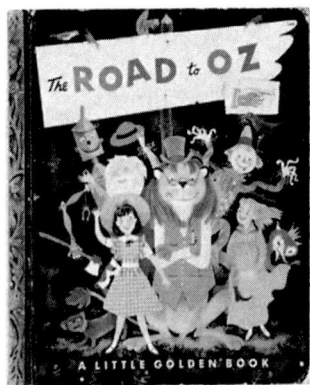

PLATE 120
(Page 134)

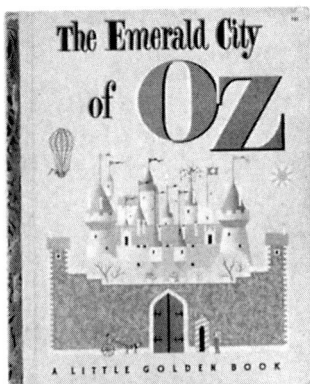

PLATE 121
(Page 134)

PLATE 122
(Page 134)

PLATE 123
(Page 136)

PLATE 124
(Page 136)

PLATE 125
(Page 136)

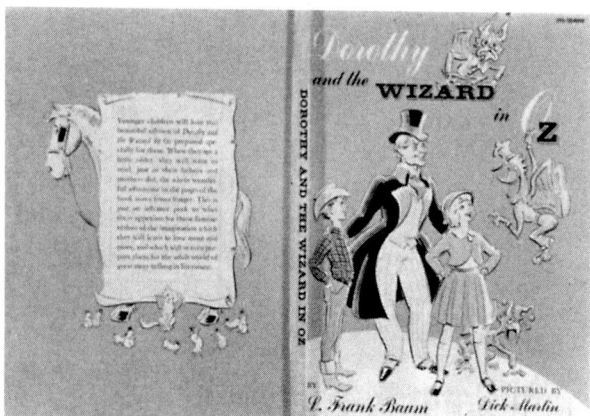

PLATE 126
(Page 136)

PLATE 127
(Page 138)

PLATE 128
(Page 138)

PLATE 129
(Page 138)

PLATE 130
(Page 138)

PLATE 131
(Page 139)

PLATE 132
(Page 139)

PLATE 133
(Page 140)

PLATE 134
(Page 140)

PLATE 135
(Page 140)

PLATE 136
(Page 140)

Later Printings

2. *Textual points*: Same as #1 except that there is a
   publisher's advertisement on the verso of the ownership
   leaf listing titles through *The Tin Woodman of Oz* (1918).

Color plates: Same as #1.

Cover: Same as #1 except that the book is bound in olive-
   green cloth.

SECONDARY BINDING: Copies of #2 sheets, including the
Reilly & Britton title page, have been seen in olive-green
cloth with "Reilly ǀ & Lee" on the spine.

Subsequent printings of *Rinkitink in Oz* carry the Reilly
& Lee imprint on the title page. The earliest of them has a
publisher's advertisement through *The Tin Woodman of Oz*
(1918) and has no captions on the color plates. Some copies
with advertisements through *Glinda of Oz* (1920) have no
color-plate captions; others have captions added to the color
plates as do later printings without advertisements. Around
1935, the color plates were discontinued; for a brief period
around this time copies were issued with a single color plate
tipped in as a frontispiece.

XI. THE LOST PRINCESS OF OZ

The Lost Princess of Oz. Chicago: The Reilly & Britton Co.,
[1917]. 312 pages. Illustrated by John R. Neill. First edition,
two states:

1. *Textual points*: The publisher's advertisement on the
   verso of the ownership leaf lists ten titles; the last is *The
   Lost Princess of Oz*. Pictorial self-endpapers in black and
   white.

Color plates: 12 full-color inserts with no captions, tipped in
   facing the title page and pages 48, 72, 104, 128, 156,
   200, 212, 224, 256, 264, 308.

Cover: (Plate 47) light-blue cloth, with a pictorial paper label in colors on the front. There are horizontal double rules at the top and bottom of the spine. The publisher's imprint on the spine reads: "Reilly & | Britton".

Dust jacket: Issued in a full-color dust jacket with an identical illustration on the front and back which reproduces the label design. The front and back flaps are blank.

Size of leaf: 8 7/8 by 6 5/8 inches. *Thickness of volume:* 1 3/8 inches.

An issue with the imprint of the Copp, Clark Co., Limited, of Toronto on the spine and title page is known. In all other respects it is identical with the American first state. One copy has been seen with the Copp, Clark imprint on the title page but with the Reilly & Britton spine imprint.

Later Printings

2. *Textual points:* Same as #1 except that the publisher's advertisement lists titles through *The Tin Woodman of Oz* (1918).

Color plates: Same as #1.

Cover: This state has been noted in various colors of cloth, including tan with a horizontal double rule at the top of the spine only, tan, light blue, and dark green, all without rules on the spine.

SECONDARY BINDING: Copies made up of #2 sheets, including the Reilly & Britton title page, have been seen bound in light-brown cloth with the publisher's name on the spine: "Reilly | & Lee".

All known subsequent printings of *The Lost Princess of Oz* carry the Reilly & Lee imprint. Copies have been reported with advertisements through *The Tin Woodman of Oz*, without captions, and through *Glinda of Oz* (1920), both with and without captions on the color plates. Later printings with no advertisements have captions on the plates. Around 1935, the color plates were discontinued; briefly at about that time, copies were issued with a single color plate as a frontispiece.

XII. THE TIN WOODMAN OF OZ

The Tin Woodman of Oz. Chicago: The Reilly & Britton Co., [1918]. 288 pages. Illustrated by John R. Neill. First edition:

Textual points: The publisher's advertisement on the verso of the ownership leaf lists eleven titles; the last is *The Tin Woodman of Oz*. Inserted pictorial endpapers in black and white.

Color plates: 12 full-color inserts with no captions, tipped in facing the title page and pages 24, 40, 72, 112, 152, 168, 192, 224, 240, 272, 280.

Cover: (Plate 48) red cloth, with a pictorial paper label in colors on the front. The publisher's imprint on the spine reads: "Reilly &   Britton".

Dust jacket: Issued in a full-color dust jacket with an identical illustration on the front and back which reproduces the label design. The front flap has a blurb for the book. The back flap advertises *Let's Write a Story*.

Size of leaf: 9 by 6 3/4 inches. *Thickness of volume*: 1 3/8 inches.

An issue with the imprint of the Copp, Clark Co., Limited, of Toronto on the title page and spine is known. It is otherwise identical with the American first state.

Later Printings

Apparently there was only one printing of *The Tin Woodman of Oz* issued by Reilly & Britton; in 1919 the firm changed its name to Reilly & Lee. The earliest Reilly & Lee printing has the same advertisements as the first state (listing through *The Tin Woodman of Oz*) and the color plates are without captions. Some copies with advertisements through *Glinda of Oz* (1920) have no color plate captions; others have captions added to the color plates, as do later printings with advertisements through *The Cowardly Lion of Oz* (1923) and still later printings without advertisements. Around 1935, the color plates were discontinued.

In 1940 an oversize "Popular Edition" (size of leaf: 9 3/8 by 7 inches) appeared (plate 49), and in 1955 Reilly & Lee selected *The Tin Woodman of Oz* for an experiment in modernization: a new, completely reset edition with illustrations by Dale Ulrey was published (cover and dust jacket, plates 50-51). It was not successful, and plans for re-illustrating the rest of the Baum Oz titles were abandoned after only two Ulrey-illustrated Oz books were published (the other was *The Wizard of Oz*, 1956). In 1965, when the book was reprinted in the uniform "white-cover" printings, the Neill illustrations and original typesetting were restored.

XIII. THE MAGIC OF OZ

The Magic of Oz. Chicago: The Reilly & Lee Co., [1919]. 266 pages. Illustrated by John R. Neill. First edition, three states:

1. *Textual points*: The publisher's advertisement on the verso of the ownership page lists eleven titles; the last is *The Tin Woodman of Oz*. Pictorial self-endpapers in black and white.

   Color plates: 12 full-color inserts with no captions, tipped in facing the title page and pages 28, 48, 64, 88, 120, 136, 142, 160, 208, 236, 248.

   Cover: (Plate 52) bound in various shades of green cloth. The following have been seen: light tannish-green, light gray-green, lime green, mint-green, and bright emerald-green. There is no known priority. On the front is a pictorial paper label in colors. The publisher's spine imprint reads: "Reilly ⏐ & Lee". The word "Reilly measures 7/8 inch in length.

Dust jacket: Issued in a full-color dust jacket with an identical illustration on the front and back which reproduces the label design. The front flap has a blurb for the book. The back flap is blank.

Size of leaf: 8 7/8 by 6 5/8 inches. *Thickness of volume*: 1 3/8 inches.

An issue with the imprint of the Copp, Clark Co., Limited, of Toronto on the title page and spine is known. In all other respects it is identical with the American first state in bright emerald-green cloth.

2. *Textual points*: Same as #1 except that the publisher's advertisement lists twelve titles; the last is *The Magic of Oz* which has been added in a different type, possibly during the first press run.

Color plates: Same as #1.

Cover: Same as #1. This state has been seen in tannish-green cloth and in olive-green cloth.

Later Printings

3. *Textual points*: Same as #s 1 and 2 except that the publisher's advertisement lists titles through *Glinda of Oz* (1920).

Color plates: Same as #s 1 and 2.

Cover: Three cloth colors noted: light blue, light drab-green, and mint-green. The publisher's name on the spine is in much larger type: "Reilly" measures 1 1/4 inches in length.

All known subsequent printings of *The Magic of Oz* with color plates contain no publisher's advertisements and have the publisher's imprint on the spine in the larger type. Most of the plates are bound in rather than tipped in. Around 1935, the color plates were discontinued.

XIV. GLINDA OF OZ

Glinda of Oz. Chicago: The Reilly & Lee Co., [1920]. 279 pages. Illustrated by John R. Neill. First edition:

Textual points: The publisher's advertisement on the verso of the half-title page lists thirteen titles; the last is *Glinda of Oz*. On page [280] is an advertisement for the *Oz-Man Tales* series. Pictorial self-endpapers in black and white.

Color plates: 12 full-color inserts with no captions, tipped in facing the title page and pages 44, 100, 108, 140, 152, 164, 172, [212], 244, 260, 276.

Cover: (Plate 53) various colors of cloth: red, brick-red, blue, gray, dark green, dull medium green, light green, light brown, and tan have been observed. No priority has been established. The fact that copies with Christmas 1920 inscriptions have been found in most of the colors suggests that all colors were issued simultaneously. On the front is a pictorial paper label in colors. The publisher's name on the spine reads: "Reilly | & Lee".

Dust jacket: Issued in a full-color dust jacket with an identical illustration on the front and back which reproduces the label design. The front flap has a blurb for the book. The back flap lists the Oz books through *Glinda of Oz*.

Size of leaf: 9 by 6 5/8 inches. *Thickness of volume*: 1 1/2 inches.

Several copies are known with the Copp, Clark Co,. Limited, of Toronto imprint on the spine and title page. Otherwise they are identical with the American first state in light-brown cloth.

Later Printings

Later printings with color plates have been seen with publisher's advertisements in the front listing titles through *The Cowardly Lion of Oz* (1923) and through *The Hungry Tiger of Oz* (1926); printings which are probably still later have no advertisements in the front. Around 1935, the color plates were discontinued.

ADDENDA—L. FRANK BAUM

The publication of *The Marvelous Land of Oz* in July 1904 began a great deal of Oz-related activity by Baum and his publishers. The next month, "Queer Visitors from the Marvelous Land of Oz," a weekly series of twenty-seven stories about the adventures of the Oz characters in the United States, began publication in various Sunday newspapers. In June 1905, Reilly & Britton published *The Woggle-Bug Book* to coincide with the opening of *The Woggle-Bug*, Baum's musical extravaganza based on the second Oz book. *The Woggle-Bug Book* is an expansion of a subplot of the play, but it is presented so as to continue the adventures of the "Queer Visitors;" it begins, "One day Mr. H.M. Woggle-Bug, T.E., becoming separated from the comrades who had accompanied him from the Land of Oz . . . ."

THE WOGGLE-BUG BOOK

The Woggle-Bug Book. Chicago: The Reilly & Britton Co., 1905. 48 pages. Illustrated by Ike Morgan. First edition:

Textual points: The book is wire side-stitched (stapled) rather than sewn in gatherings. There are no endpapers; the first page is the title page. The text throughout the book is printed in dark blue. Beginning with page 4, the text is printed on even numbered pages only, against background panels printed in pale yellow at the top fading to pale pink at the bottom. This colored panel is bordered at the top and along the left edge with a frieze consisting of the heads of major characters in the story, printed in full color on pale-blue panels. Each odd-numbered page contains one or more illustrations in full color. Page [48] concludes with a blurb for *The Marvelous Land of Oz*, and just below the background panel is a horizontal rule and a colophon statement: "PRESS OF STEARNS BROTHERS & CO., CHICAGO".

Cover: (Plate 54) paper-covered boards, with a spine strip of plain green cloth. The front cover is printed in colors, with a background field of gray-green. This field's color was achieved by superimposing a dot-stipple printing of dark blue over a similar stippled pattern of pale yellow. The back cover is plain white cardboard with no printing. It is doubtful that the book was issued with a dust jacket.

SECONDARY BINDING: The lettering and overall design of the front cover are identical with the earlier binding case except that the blue stippled pattern has been deleted from the background field, leaving the field of pale-yellow stipple pattern. In the center of the back cover, outlined in yellow, is: "The WOGGLE-BUG | BOOK". The background is a pale yellow, dot-stippled field.

Size of leaf: 15 by 11 1/4 inches. *Thickness of volume*: 1/4 inch.

NOTE: Classification of the two states of the cover of *The Woggle-Bug Book* was first determined by Dick Martin, who published the original description of the book in *The Baum Bugle*, Christmas 1969: "Although the state with the blank back cover might seem to be the later one, in keeping with Reilly & Britton's frequent cost-cutting omissions of later years, the above priority is suggested by the fact that the difference between the gray-green and pale yellow fields of the front cover is a *subtractive* one: examination of the pale-yellow state shows some raggedness on the outline of the heart and on some of the lettering, indicating traces of the blue half-tone dots incompletely etched out. In other words, the blue half-toning appears to have been removed rather than added, possibly to give a lighter and brighter appearance to the design."

Later Printings

In 1978, an edition with an introduction by Douglas G. Greene was published by Scholars' Facsimiles & Reprints of Delmar, New York. It contains photographic reproductions of the original text and illustrations, in black and white and in reduced size; page size is approximately 8 1/2 by 5 3/8 inches. The book is bound in tan cloth, lettered on the spine in black. The introduction reproduces a drawing for the book by Ike Morgan which did not appear in the 1905 edition; it was first printed in *The Baum Bugle*, Christmas 1969. A second printing of this edition appeared in 1982. See also *The Third Book of Oz*, described below.

THE VISITORS FROM OZ

This volume is loosely based on eleven of the episodes of Baum's newspaper series "Queer Visitors from the Marvelous Land of Oz" (1904-1905). Jean Kellogg's adaptation of the original stories does not preserve much of Baum's language, and the book has been described as only "attributed to L. Frank Baum."

The Visitors from Oz. Chicago: The Reilly & Lee Co., [1960]. 95 pages. "Adapted for today's children" [by Jean Kellogg]. Illustrated by Dick Martin. First edition:

Textual points: The book is side-stitched rather than sewn in gatherings. Printed so that throughout the book a double-page spread of color pictures is followed by a double-page spread of black-and-white pictures. Blank lining papers pasted to the inside of the covers.

Cover: (Plate 55) imprinted white cloth, with illustrations on the front and back in full color. (The background color is green).

Dust jacket: Issued in a full-color dust jacket that reproduces the design used on the book's cover. Printed on white, coated stock. The front flap has a blurb for *The Visitors from Oz,* and the back flap lists the section headings for the various episodes in the story.

Size of leaf: 11 by 8 3/8 inches. *Thickness of volume:* 1/2 inch. Copies in the secondary bindings are normally thicker and the pages have been trimmed to a smaller size.

SECONDARY BINDINGS:*The Visitors from Oz* occurs in two different binding-cases produced primarily for libraries, although B was also available for sale to the general public.

A) Blue-green cloth. The front cover has a slightly reduced, full-color reproduction of the original front cover design; the back cover is blank. This binding-case was manufactured by a specialist firm that produced such covers for purchase by libraries and book-distributors that chose to have their own binders recase the books.

B) Bright-green, yellow, or red buckram cloth. The front cover has a redrawn version of the original front cover design, silk-screened in black and white; the back cover is blank except for the imprint of American Publishers Company.

THE THIRD BOOK OF OZ

This book contains all twenty-seven episodes of "Queer Visitors from the Marvelous Land of Oz." The only major textual change is that the episodes that ended with a question for the "What Did the Woggle-Bug Say?" newspaper contest, now end with the answers included in the final line. The book also includes the text for *The Woggle-Bug Book.*

The Third Book of Oz. [Savannah: Armstrong State College Press, 1986]. [xii] + 165 pages. Edited by Martin Williams. Illustrated by Eric Shanower. First edition, two states:

1. *Textual points*: "Perfect-bound," that is, the book is made up of single leaves held together at the spine with glue.

Cover: (Plate 56) yellow stiff-paper wrappers, trimmed to page size and printed on the front, back, and spine in black. The front cover reproduces the title page.

Size of leaf: 10 7/8 by 8 3/8 inches. *Thickness of volume*: approximately 9/16 inch.

2. Same as #1 except that the book is printed on heavier paper-stock so that it is approximately 1 inch thick.

THE LITTLE WIZARD SERIES

In 1913, L. Frank Baum and Reilly & Britton brought out the first Oz book in three years, *The Patchwork Girl of Oz.* The hiatus in the series had resulted from Baum's attempt to begin the Trot and Cap'n Bill series with *The Sea Fairies* (1911) and *Sky Island* (1912). It soon became clear that readers preferred Oz, and Baum devoted himself to re-establishing the Oz series. Perhaps to appeal to younger readers who had not yet discovered Oz, six short Oz stories were published in 1913 as *The Little Wizard Series.*

The Little Wizard Series. Six small volumes: *The Cowardly Lion and the Hungry Tiger, Little Dorothy and Toto, Tiktok* [sic] *and the Nome King, Ozma and the Little Wizard, Jack Pumpkinhead and the Sawhorse,* and *The Scarecrow and the Tin Woodman.* Chicago: The Reilly & Britton Co., [1913]. 29 pages in each volume. [Illustrated by John R. Neill.] First edition:

Textual points: Bound in a single gathering, saddle wire-stitched (stapled in the center). The text is printed in blue

on a slightly rough wove paper stock. The title page is
printed in blue and red. There are no color plates, but the
textual illustrations are printed in full color. Pictorial self-
endpapers, with the shadowed areas below the lion and
the tiger printed in blue half-tone stipple.

NOTE: In the first edition of *Bibliographia Oziana*, two
states were described with priority undetermined. It is
now clear that what was then called state B is the standard
form of the volumes, and thus it is described above under
"textual points." State A differs in being printed on highly
calendered, semi-glossy paper stock, with the shadowed
areas below the lion and the tiger on the endpapers printed
in solid blue. A recent census of copies of *The Little
Wizard Series* located more than eighty examples of state
B, but only one of state A, a copy of *The Cowardly Lion and
the Hungry Tiger* which was once owned by L. Frank
Baum's widow. The status of this book is undetermined,
though it may be a preliminary, experimental, or proof
copy.

Covers: (Plates 57-62) pictorial, paper-covered boards,
printed in colors. It is unlikely that the series was issued
in dust jackets.

Size of leaf: 6 13/16 by 5 5/16 inches. *Thickness of each
volume*: 3/16 inch.

Later Printings

[*The Little Wizard Series*] *The Little Oz Books with Jig
Saw Oz Puzzles*. Two boxed sets (plates 63-64) each
containing two of *The Little Wizard Series* books and two
jigsaw puzzles (reproduced from the center-spread illustration
of each book): set 1 contains *Ozma and the Little Wizard*
and *The Scarecrow and the Tin Woodman*; set 2 contains
Tiktok and the Nome King and *Jack Pumpkinhead and the
Sawhorse*. Chicago: The Reilly & Lee Co., [1932].

Textual points: On the verso of the title page is an advertisement for the two jigsaw puzzle sets. Bound in a single gathering, saddle wire-stitched (stapled in the center). The text is printed in black, and the reset title page is in black and red; text illustrations are in color. The shadowed areas below the lion and tiger at front and back of *Tiktok and the Nome King* are in black stipple; the other three booklets have solid black shadows.

Covers: Paper wrappers with designs the same as the 1913 printings, except that the front cover caption "LITTLE WIZARD SERIES" has been deleted.

Size of leaf: Varies slightly but approximately 7 1/16 by 5 3/16 inches. *Thickness of volume*: 1/8 inch.

[*The Little Wizard Series*] The Jell-O booklets: Four volumes: *Ozma and the Little Wizard, Tiktok and the Nome King, Jack Pumpkinhead and the Sawhorse,* and *The Scarecrow and the Tin Woodman*. Chicago: The Reilly & Lee Co., [1932].

Textual points: On the verso of the title page, page [30], and the inside back cover are Jell-O advertisements and dessert recipes. Bound in a single gathering, saddle wire-stitched (stapled in the center). The text is printed in black, and the title page is in black and red; text illustrations are in color. The shadowed areas below the lion and tiger at front are solid black.

Covers: (Plate 65) paper wrappers with designs the same as the 1913 printings, except that the front-cover caption "LITTLE WIZARD SERIES" has been deleted, and the back cover contains a drawing of the Scarecrow and Tin Woodman carrying a giant dish of Jell-O.

Size of leaf: 6 1/2 by 4 7/8 inches. *Thickness of volume*: 1/8 inch.

[*The Little Wizard Series*] *The Wonderful Land of Oz Library*: Three volumes: *Little Dorothy and Toto of Oz, also The Cowardly Lion and the Hungry Tiger of Oz; Jack Pumpkinhead and the Sawhorse of Oz, also Tik-tok* [sic] *and the Gnome* [sic] *King of Oz*; and *The Scarecrow and the Tin Woodman of Oz, also Princess Ozma of Oz*. Chicago: Rand McNally & Company, [1939]. 61 pages in first two volumes; 64 pages in the last.

These three books contain the six *Little Wizard* stories in reset type. Page size is 6 3/8 by 5 1/4 inches. The volumes are bound in pictorial paper-covered boards, printed in color (plate 66). The first printing has "CS 3-39" below the copyright notice on the verso of the title page. These three volumes and six abridgments of the larger Oz books comprise *The Wonderful Land of Oz Library*. (See below, pp. 133-134).

In 1942, Hutchinson of London reprinted two of the *Little Wizard* booklets, now entitled *Princess Ozma of Oz* and *Scarecrow and the Tin Woodman of Oz*, with some of the Neill illustrations, redrawn in black and white. They are oversize volumes (size of leaf: 13 by 8 1/8 inches) and bound in stiff paper with new cover designs by another artist (plates 67-68).

LITTLE WIZARD STORIES OF OZ

This book contains all six of *The Little Wizard Series* with the Neill illustrations in color.

Little Wizard Stories of Oz. Chicago: The Reilly & Britton Co., [1914]. Approximately 196 pages.* Illustrated by John R. Neill [with ownership leaf by Maginel Wright Enright from Baum's pseudonymous *Policeman Bluejay* (1907)]. First edition, two states:

---

* The pagination of this book is extremely jumbled. The page numerals of the six separate volumes were left unchanged, so that the last page number in the collected edition is 29. Further confusion is created by the fact that the full-page illustrations (which were included in the original pagination and had text pages on the versos) are here printed with blank versos.

1. *Textual points*: Printed on smooth paper stock. The text and title page are printed in blue; illustrations are in color. At the end of the book is an advertisement for the Oz series through *The Patchwork Girl of Oz*. Pictorial self-endpapers with the same design as those in the six *Little Wizard* booklets; the shadowed areas are stippled.

Cover: (Plate 69) yellow-orange cloth. Pictorial paper label in colors. The spine is stamped in red, with "Reilly & | Britton" at the foot.

Dust jacket: Issued in a full-color dust jacket with an illustration on the front which reproduces the label design. The back reproduces in reduced size the advertisement on the verso of the half-title page from *Tik-Tok of Oz* (1914). The front flap has a blurb for the book. The back flap has a blurb for *Tik-Tok of Oz*.

Size of leaf: About 7 1/2 by 5 3/4 inches. *Thickness of volume*: 1 inch.

Later Printings

2. *Textual points*: Printed on a rougher paper stock. The book is about 1 1/8 inches thick.

Cover: Same as #1. Copies have been reported both in first-state dust jackets and in dust jackets with advertisements for other books printed in 1916.

SECONDARY BINDING: Buff or tan cloth. It seems likely that copies in this binding represent a third printing.

In 1985, an edition with an introduction by Michael Patrick Hearn was published by Schocken Books of New York. It contains the original illustrations in full color. The type has been reset, and new, correct page numerals added; this edition has 145 pages. It is bound in red cloth, lettered in gilt.

THE OZ BOOKS OF RUTH PLUMLY THOMPSON

After a long illness, L. Frank Baum died in May 1919. *The Magic of Oz* was already in press, and Baum had completed the manuscript for *Glinda of Oz*. Sometime in 1920, Reilly & Lee entered a contract with Baum's widow, Maud G. Baum, and Ruth Plumly Thompson to continue the Oz series. Under the contract Mrs. Baum received royalty payments on the Oz books written by Thompson.

Despite comments in the forewords to *Glinda of Oz* and *The Royal Book of Oz* that suggest Baum had left notes for an unfinished Oz book and that Thompson had "enlarged and edited" those notes to create *The Royal Book of Oz*, the story was entirely the work of Ruth Plumly Thompson. Not until the 1985 Del Rey/Ballantine edition was Thompson credited as author on the cover and title page of the book.

XV. THE ROYAL BOOK OF OZ

The Royal Book of Oz. Chicago: The Reilly & Lee Co., [1921]. 303 pages. Illustrated by John R. Neill. First edition:

Textual points: Pictorial self-endpapers in black and white. Pages 305-312 contain publisher's advertisements for the Oz series; these advertisements were retained in reprints of the book for many years.

Color plates: 12 full-color inserts, some tipped in, some bound in. The plates are printed on stock coated only on the printed side. The plate facing the title page is tipped in; bound-in plates facing pages 30 and 47, 78 and 95, 126 and 143, 174 and 191, 238 and 255; the final plate is tipped in facing page 286. The caption on the plate facing page 255 has a misprint: "SCARECORW'S" for "SCARECROW'S".

Cover: (Plate 70) light-gray cloth, with pictorial paper label in colors. Spine imprint reads: "Reilly ┃ & Lee".

Size of leaf: 9 by 6 1/2 inches. *Thickness of volume*: 1 3/8 inches.

An issue with the imprint of the Copp, Clark Co., Limited, of Toronto on the title page and spine is known. It is otherwise identical with the American first state.

Later Printings

Subsequent color-plate printings correct the misprint on the plate facing page 255. The four plates facing pages 126, 143, 174, and 191 have been relocated so that they face pages 142, 159, 190, and 207. The earliest of the later printings is also bound in light-gray cloth with the plates printed on stock coated only on the printed side. Later states are bound in dark-gray, gray-green, or blue cloth. They have plates of stock coated on both sides. Around 1935, the color plates were discontinued.

XVI. KABUMPO IN OZ

Kabumpo in Oz. Chicago: The Reilly & Lee Co., [1922]. 297 pages. Illustrated by John R. Neill. First edition:

Textual points: What are almost certainly the earliest copies have a half-title following the ownership leaf: an elephant with "KABUMPO ┃ IN OZ" lettered on his robe ("OZ" is a stylized device with the "Z" within the "O"). A portrait of Princess Dorothy appears on page [299]. Pictorial self-endpapers in black and white.

Color plates: 12 full-color inserts, some tipped in, some bound in: tipped-in plate facing title page; bound-in plates facing pages 57 and 72, 105 and 120, 153 and 168, 217 and 232, 249 and 264; tipped-in plate facing 288. The plates are coated only on the printed side.

Cover: (Plate 71) blue or blue-green cloth, with pictorial paper label in colors. Spine imprint reads: "Reilly | & Lee".

Size of leaf: 9 by 6 5/8 inches. *Thickness of volume:* 1 1/2 inches.

An issue with the imprint of the Copp, Clark Co., Limited, of Toronto on the title page and the spine is known. It is otherwise identical with the American first state in blue-green cloth.

Later Printings

The half-title of later copies is at the end of the book, and the portrait of Dorothy follows the ownership leaf.* The earliest reprint (ca. 1923) has been reported in green cloth and in a blue-green cloth which is greener than the first state, and it has a non-standard ampersand, &, instead of the usual & in the publisher's imprint on the spine. Later states (again with the standard ampersand) have been noted in very dark blue and in medium-blue cloth, with plates coated only on the printed side. Still later copies in various colors of cloth and of varying thickness have plates coated on both sides. Around 1935, the color plates were discontinued.

XVII. THE COWARDLY LION OF OZ

The Cowardly Lion of Oz. Chicago: The Reilly & Lee Co., [1923]. 291 pages. Illustrated by John R. Neill. First edition:

Textual points: The book is made up of 16-page gatherings except for a terminal gathering of 8 pages. Pictorial self-endpapers in black and white.

---

*This reversal did not necessarily require a separate printing; as the first and last gatherings of the book contain only 8 pages each, undoubtedly printed on the same sheet, alternate methods of cutting and folding could have resulted in the transposition. The other gatherings all have 16 pages.

Color plates: 12 full-color inserts, some tipped in, some bound in : tipped-in plate facing title page; bound-in plates facing pages 32 and 49, 96 and 113, 144 and 161, 208 and 225, 256 and 273; final plate tipped in facing page 280. Plates are on stock coated only on the printed side.

Cover: (Plate 72) deep emerald-green or drab-green (textured) cloth, with pictorial paper label in colors and with a non-standard ampersand, &, instead of the usual & in the publisher's imprint on the spine: "Reilly | & Lee".

SECONDARY BINDING: A secondary binding on first-state sheets has been observed. It is in very dark green cloth, with the standard ampersand, &, in the spine imprint.

Size of leaf: 9 by 6 5/8 inches. *Thickness of volume*: varies between 1 3/8 and 1 1/2 inches.

The Cowardly Lion of Oz appeared with the Canadian imprint of the Copp, Clark Co., Limited, of Toronto. Except for the publisher's imprint on the title page and spine, it is identical with the American first state, bound in deep emerald-green cloth. One color-plate copy, apparently manufactured in the bindery, has the Canadian spine imprint and a cancel Reilly & Lee title page.

Later Printings

All subsequent printings with color plates have the standard ampersand on the spine and a terminal gathering of 24 pages. The earliest of these re-imposed copies is bound in very dark green with plates coated only on the printed side. Later copies bound in medium green have been seen with plates coated only on the printed side and with plates coated on both sides. Around 1935, the color plates were discontinued.

XVIII. GRAMPA IN OZ

Grampa in Oz. Chicago: The Reilly & Lee Co., [1924]. 271 pages. Illustrated by John R. Neill. First edition:

Textual points: The book is printed on heavy paper stock and measures approximately 1 7/16 inches thick. The four pages (each with a blank verso) of advertisements at the end of the book were included without change in subsequent printings for many years. Pictorial self-endpapers in black and white.*

Color plates: 12 full-color inserts, bound in (there is no color frontispiece: a black-and-white picture which is part of the text sheets faces the title page) facing pages 28 and 45, 76 and 93, 124 and 141, 172 and 189, 220 and 237, 252 and [269]. Stock coated only on the printed side.

Cover: (Plate 73) light brick-red cloth, with pictorial paper label in colors. Spine imprint: "Reilly ǀ & Lee".

Size of leaf: 9 by 6 5/8 inches.

An issue with the imprint of the Copp, Clark Co., Limited, of Toronto on the title page and spine is known. It is otherwise identical with the American first state.

Later Printings

Later printings are on thinner paper stock and differ somewhat in binding colors. Copies have been seen in light and dark brick-red cloth (each about 1 5/16 inches thick) with plates coated only on the printed side; in dark brick-red cloth (1 3/16 inches thick) with various combinations of plates coated on only the printed side and on both sides, and in brick-red cloth lighter than the first-state binding (1 1/8 inches thick) with all plates coated on both sides. Around 1935, the color plates were discontinued, but for a brief time copies were issued with only 2 color plates.

---

*All copies of the first printing examined have perfect type in the numeral on page 171 and in the last word in the next-to-last line on page 189. All copies of later printings examined show type damage in these two places.

XIX. THE LOST KING OF OZ

The Lost King of Oz. Chicago: The Reilly & Lee Co., [1925]. 280 pages. Illustrated by John R. Neill. First edition:

Textual points: The book is printed on heavy paper stock and measures about 1 3/8 inches thick. Pictorial self-endpapers in black and white.*

Color plates: 12 full-color inserts, tipped in facing the title page and pages 14, 46, 62, 78, 94, 110, 158, 174, 222, 238, 270. The plates are printed on stock coated only on the printed side.

Cover: (Plate 74) medium-blue cloth, with pictorial paper label in colors. Spine imprint reads in boldface type: "Reilly │ & Lee".

Size of leaf: 9 by 6 5/8 inches.

An issue with the imprint of the Copp, Clark Co., Limited, of Toronto on the title page and spine is known. It is otherwise identical with the American first state; copies of the Canadian issue have been seen both with perfect type and with damaged type as described in the footnote below.

Later Printings

Later printings vary primarily in the coating and method of inserting the color plates. The earliest reprints are in deep royal-blue cloth with all the plates tipped in and coated on both sides. Subsequent printings have all the plates bound in and coated on both sides, although two transitional copies have been seen: one in deep royal-blue cloth with 6 tipped-in and 6 bound-in plates, and one in bright-blue cloth with 10 tipped-in and 2 bound-in plates. The last color-plate printing (ca. 1934) in bright-blue cloth has the publisher's name on

*What may be the earliest copies of the first printing have the letter "k" page 193, line 4, perfect. Other copies apparently from the same press run have the top serif of that letter missing.

the spine in semi-script, "fancy" letters. It is in a thinner format (about 1 1/4 inches thick). Around 1935, the color plates were discontinued.

XX. THE HUNGRY TIGER OF OZ

The Hungry Tiger of Oz. Chicago: The Reilly & Lee Co., [1926]. 261 pages. Illustrated by John R. Neill. First edition:

Textual points: The two pages (each with a blank verso) of advertisements at the end of the book were included without charge in all printings for many years. Pictorial self-endpapers in black and white.*

Color plates: 12 full-color inserts, tipped in facing the title page and pages 32, 64, 72, 128, 136, 152, 200, 216, 224, 240, 256. Plate stock is coated only on the printed side.

Cover: (Plate 75) dark drab-green cloth with pictorial paper label in colors. Spine imprint: "Reilly ⏐ & Lee".

Size of leaf: 9 by 6 5/8 inches. *Thickness of volume*: About 1 3/8 inches.

An issue with the imprint of the Copp, Clark Co., Limited, of Toronto on the title page and spine is known. It is otherwise identical with the American first state.

Later Printings

Later states have color plates coated on both sides. Such copies have been seen in dark emerald-green, medium-green, and medium brick-red cloth. Around 1935, the color plates were discontinued.

---

*What may be the earliest copies of the first printing have the hyphen on the last line, page 21, and the word "two", last line of page 252, in perfect type. Other copies apparently from the same press run have damaged type in one or both places.

XXI. THE GNOME KING OF OZ

The Gnome King of Oz. Chicago: The Reilly & Lee Co.,
[1927]. 282 pages. Illustrated by John R. Neill. First edition:

Textual points: Pictorial self-endpapers in black and white.

Color plates: 12 full-color inserts, tipped in facing the title
   page and pages 46, 78, 94, 102, 126, 158, 174, 190, 206,
   222, 278. Plate stock is coated on both sides.

Cover: (Plate 76) bright emerald-green or light jade-green
   cloth, with pictorial paper label in colors. (Although
   priority is not firmly established, contemporary inscrip-
   tions indicate that the light jade-green copies are later.)
   Spine imprint: "Reilly ⎸ & Lee".

Size of leaf: 8 7/8 by 6 5/8 inches. *Thickness of volume*:
   1 1/4 inches.

An issue with the imprint of the Copp, Clark Co.,
Limited, of Toronto on the title page and spine is known. It is
otherwise identical with the American first state in bright
emerald-green cloth. The publisher's imprint at the foot of
the Canadian title page is known in two forms. Variant 1 has
only a period between "Co" and "Limited"; variant 2 has a
period and a comma between those words. There is no known
priority.

Later Printings

Although there were probably several printings of this
book with color plates, no variants have been identified.
Around 1935, the color plates were discontinued.

XXII. THE GIANT HORSE OF OZ

The Giant Horse of Oz. Chicago and New York: The Reilly
& Lee Co., [1928]. 281 pages. Illustrated by John R. Neill.
First edition:

Textual points: Pictorial self-endpapers in black and white.*
Pages 126 and 127 are printed in the correct order.

Color plates: 12 full-color inserts, tipped in facing title page
and pages 48, 64, 80, 128, 160, 192, 208, 224, 240, 248,
272. The plate stock is coated only on the printed side.
The frontispiece has a misprint: "ONIBERON" for "QUIBER-
ON".

Cover: (Plate 77) brick-red cloth, with pictorial paper label
in colors. Spine imprint: "Reilly | & Lee".

Size of leaf: 8 7/8 by 6 5/8 inches. *Thickness of volume*:
1 1/4 inches.

A Canadian issue appeared with the imprint of the Copp,
Clark Co., Limited, of Toronto. Except for the publisher's
imprint on the title page and spine, it is identical with the first
American state.

Later Printings

Later copies, bound in the same color as the first state and
in a darker brick-red cloth, correct the frontispiece misprint
and have plates printed on stock coated on both sides; the
order of pages 126 and 127 has been inverted. Around 1935,
the color plates were discontinued. All copies examined without color plates have restored the correct order to pages 126-
127.

XXIII. JACK PUMPKINHEAD OF OZ

Jack Pumpkinhead of Oz. Chicago and New York: The
Reilly & Lee Co., [1929]. 252 pages. Illustrated by John R.
Neill. First edition:

Textual points: 16-page gatherings except the penultimate,
which has 24 pages. The two pages (each with blank

---

*What may be the earliest copies of the first printing have the "r" in "morning",
page 116, line 1, undamaged. Other copies apparently from the same press run have
damaged type here.

verso) of advertisements at the end of the book were included without change in all printings for many years. Pictorial self-endpapers in black and white.

Color plates: 12 full-color inserts, some tipped in and some bound in: the plate facing the title page is tipped in; bound-in plates face pages 64 and 81, 96 and 113, 160 and 177, 192 and 209, 228 and 245, with another plate tipped in facing page 237. Plate stock is coated on both sides. (One copy has been reported with 3 of the plates coated only on the printed side.)

Cover: (Plate 78) greenish-gray or very light-gray cloth, with pictorial paper label in colors. Spine imprint: "Reilly & Lee".

Size of leaf: 9 by 6 5/8 inches. *Thickness of volume*: 1 1/4 inches.

An issue with the imprint of the Copp, Clark Co., Limited, of Toronto on the title page and spine is known. It is otherwise identical with the first American state. One copy has been seen with the Copp, Clark imprint on the title page but with the Reilly & Lee spine imprint.

Later Printings

Although there were probably several printings of this book with color plates, no variants have been identified. Around 1935, the color plates were discontinued.

XXIV. THE YELLOW KNIGHT OF OZ

The Yellow Knight of Oz. Chicago and New York: The Reilly & Lee Co., [1930]. 275 pages. Illustrated by John R. Neill. First edition:

Textual points: 16-page gatherings except the penultimate, which has 24 pages. Pictorial self-endpapers in black and white.

Color plates: 12 full-color inserts, tipped in facing the title page and pages 40, 68, 80, 104, 136, 148, 176, 200, 224, 240, 260. Plate stock is coated on both sides.

Cover: (Plate 79) the most frequently observed binding case is brick-red cloth, although copies have also been seen in rose (textured) and in mauve (textured) cloth. Pictorial paper label in colors. Spine imprint in boldface: "Reilly ⌐ & Lee".

SECONDARY BINDING: Brick-red cloth, with the publisher's imprint in the semi-script, "fancy" letters (ca. 1934).

Size of leaf: 9 by 6 58 inches. *Thickness of volume*: About 1 1/4 inches.

An issue with the imprint of the Copp, Clark Co., Limited, of Toronto on the title page and spine is known. It is otherwise identical with the first American state in brick-red cloth.

Later Printings

All copies printed after 1935 have no color plates.

XXV. PIRATES IN OZ

Pirates in Oz. Chicago: The Reilly & Lee Co., [1931]. 280 pages. Illustrated by John R. Neill. First edition:

Textual points: Pictorial self-endpapers in black and white.

Color plates: 12 full-color inserts, tipped in facing title page and pages 48, 64, 80, 104, 128, 144, 160, 176, 208, 256, 272. Printed on stock coated only on the printed side.

Cover: (Plate 80) medium-green (textured or untextured), turquoise (untextured), off-white (textured), or light olive-green (textured) cloth, with pictorial paper label in colors. Priority of the cloth colors has not been established, but there is some indication that the medium-green copies are the earliest. Spine imprint in boldface: "Reilly ⌐ & Lee".

SECONDARY BINDING: Medium-green cloth, with the spine imprint in the semi-script, "fancy" letters (ca. 1934).

Size of leaf: 9 by 6 5/8 inches. *Thickness of volume*: 1 3/8 inches.

Copies have been seen with the Canadian imprint of the Copp, Clark Co., Limited, of Toronto. With the exception of the publisher's imprint on the title page and spine, they are identical with the first state. They have medium-green, textured-cloth binding cases.

Later Printings

All copies printed after 1935 have no color plates.

XXVI. THE PURPLE PRINCE OF OZ

The Purple Prince of Oz. Chicago: The Reilly & Lee Co., [1932]. 281 pages. Illustrated by John R. Neill. First edition:

Textual points: Pictorial self-endpapers in black and white.

Color plates: 12 full-color inserts, tipped in facing the title page and pages 24, 72, 96, 128, 136, 168, 192, 200, 224, 248, 256. Plate stock coated only on the printed side.

Cover: (Plate 81) dark-purple (shades vary slightly) or light-purple cloth, wth pictorial paper label in colors. No priority is known. Spine imprint in boldface: "Reilly & Lee". The dust jacket, however, has the spine imprint in the semi-script "fancy" letters.

SECONDARY BINDING: Light-purple cloth, with the spine imprint in the semi-script, "fancy" letters (ca. 1934).

Size of leaf: 9 by 6 5/8 inches. *Thickness of volume*: 1 3/8 inches.

Later Printings

All copies printed after 1935 have no color plates.

XXVII. OJO IN OZ

Ojo in Oz. Chicago: The Reilly & Lee Co., [1933]. 304 pages. Illustrated by John R. Neill. First edition:

Textual points: Pictorial endpapers in black and white. The front endpaper is inserted; the back is a self-endpaper.

Color plates: 12 full-color inserts, tipped in facing the title page and pages 28, 52, 100, 116, 140, 156, 180, 196, 212, 244, 268. The plate stock is coated on both sides.

Cover: (Plate 82) various colors of cloth: green, blue-green, gray-green, dark gray, light blue, very dark blue, light tan, light brown, dark brown, and dark brick-red have been reported. There is no known priority among the color variants. Pictorial paper label in colors. The spine imprint reads in boldface: "Reilly | & Lee".

SECONDARY BINDINGS: Ca. 1934 copies, have been seen bound in blue, dark-red, dark blue-green, and putty-gray cloth, with the spine imprint in the semi-script, "fancy" letters.

Size of leaf: 9 by 6 5/8 inches. *Thickness of volume*: 1 1/2 inches.

Later Printings

All copies printed after 1935 have no color plates.

XXVIII. SPEEDY IN OZ

Speedy in Oz. Chicago: The Reilly & Lee Co., [1934]. 298 pages. Illustrated by John R. Neill. First edition:

Textual points: Pictorial self-endpapers in black and white.

Color plates: 12 full-color inserts, some tipped in and some bound in: plate facing the title page is tipped in; other plates face page 32 and 49 (bound in), 80 and 97 (bound in), 128 (tipped in), 160 (tipped in), 192 and 209 (bound in), 224 (tipped in), 256 (tipped in), and 288 (tipped in). The plate stock is coated only on the printed side.

Cover: (Plate 83) various color of cloth: black, dull blue (textured and untextured), medium blue, dark deep blue, gray, maroon, sage-green, olive-green, light brown, bright red, and bluish-purple (textured) cloth have been reported. Pictorial paper label in colors. The spine printing on the copies bound in black cloth is in orange; on copies in other colors the spine printing is in black. No priority is known; all color-plate copies are assumed to be the original state. On this book as on first states of subsequent books in the regular Oz series (except for *Merry Go Round in Oz*), the Reilly & Lee imprint on the spine is in the semi-script, "fancy" letters.

Size of leaf: 9 by 6 5/8 inches. *Thickness of volume*: 1 1/2 inches.

Later Printings

Later copies lack color plates. One copy, purchased new about 1938, has been reported with the publisher's imprint on the spine in boldface. It has no color plates.

XXIX. THE WISHING HORSE OF OZ

The Wishing Horse of Oz. Chicago: The Reilly & Lee Co., [1935]. 297 pages. Illustrated by John R. Neill. First edition:

Textual points: Blank self-endpapers.

Color plates: 12 full-color inserts, some bound in, some tipped in. Plates face title page (tipped in), and pages 48 and 65 (bound in), 96 (tipped in), 128 (tipped in), 160 and 177 (bound in), 192 (tipped in), 224 and 241 (bound in), 272 and 289 (bound in). The plates are coated only on the printed side.

Cover: (Plate 84) various colors of cloth have been reported including very dark green (both textured and untextured), greenish-gray (textured), light blue, medium blue, dark blue, lavender, coral, maroon (textured), dark red, and purplish-brown. Copies in coral, maroon, dark red and light, medium and dark blue have been noted with headbands of black-and-white striped fabric. Other copies have no headbands. There is no known priority among these variants; all color-plate copies are assumed to be of the first state. Pictorial paper label in colors. Spine imprint is in semi-script, "fancy" letters.

Size of leaf: 9 by 6 5/8 inches. *Thickness of volume:* 1 1/2 inches.

Later Printings

Later copies lack color plates. This is the only Reilly & Lee Oz book that never had its own illustrated endpapers, although at least one late reprint contains pictorial endpapers from *The Tin Woodman of Oz.*

XXX. CAPTAIN SALT IN OZ

Captain Salt in Oz. Chicago: The Reilly & Lee Co., [1936]. 306 pages. Illustrated by John R. Neill. First edition:

Textual points: The book is made up of 16-page gatherings except the last, which has 8 pages. Pictorial self-endpapers in black and white. (*Captain Salt in Oz* and subsequent volumes of the series were issued without color plates.)

Cover: (Plate 85) copies have been noted bound in light-blue medium-blue, vermilion, and green cloth. Priority has not been established, but the book is most commonly found in the blue shades and they may be earliest. Pictorial paper label in colors. Spine imprint in semi-script, "fancy" letters.

Size of leaf: 8 7/8 by 6 5/8 inches. *Thickness of volume:* 1 3/8 inches.

Later Printings

Later printings are made up of 32-page gatherings, except for the final of 16 pages. Some have pictorial endpapers; others do not.

XXXI. HANDY MANDY IN OZ

Handy Mandy in Oz. Chicago: The Reilly & Lee Co., [1937]. 246 pages. Illustrated by John R. Neill. First edition:

Textual points: The book is made up of 16-page gatherings. Pictorial self-endpapers in black and white.

Cover: (Plate 86) various colors of cloth have been reported, including yellow, red, orange, blue, and light blue-green. No priority is known. Pictorial paper label in colors. The spine has a picture of Handy Mandy. Spine imprint in semi-script, "fancy" letters.

Size of leaf: 9 by 6 5/8 inches. *Thickness of volume*: 1 1/4 inches.

Later Printings

Later printings are made up of 32-page gatherings. Some have pictorial endpapers; others do not. At least one late copy replaces the picture of Handy Mandy on the spine with a drawing of a fish that originally appeared on the spine of Baum's *The Sea Fairies*.

XXXII. THE SILVER PRINCESS IN OZ

The Silver Princess in Oz. Chicago: The Reilly & Lee Co., [1938]. 255 pages. Illustrated by John R. Neill. First edition:

Textual points: 16-page gatherings. Pictorial endpapers in black and white. The front endpaper is a self-endpaper; rear endpaper is inserted.

Cover: (Plate 87) various colors of cloth: vermilion, pink (textured), light brown, turquoise, yellow, orange, dark green, light blue-gray, and sky-blue have been reported. Pictorial paper label in colors, with the title, except for the Oz monogram, printed in metallic-silver ink. The spine illustration is of Handy Mandy. Spine imprint in semi-script, "fancy" letters.

SECONDARY BINDINGS: Copies have been reported in red, orange, and sky-blue cloth which are in every respect first states except that they have no spine illustration. Another copy, which also has a first-state text and pictorial label, is in a dark brick-red binding case with a picture of the Tin Woodman (taken from the spine of *Dorothy and the Wizard in Oz*) on the spine; the inserted rear endpaper is blank.

Size of leaf: 8 7/8 by 6 5/8 inches. *Thickness of volume*: About 1 3/8 inches.

Later Printings

Later printings have 32-page gatherings except the last (8 pages) and blank endpapers, and the lettering of the title on the cover label is in red. Some of these have no spine illustration; others have the illustration of Handy Mandy.

XXXIII. OZOPLANING WITH THE WIZARD OF OZ

Ozoplaning with the Wizard of Oz. Chicago: Reilly & Lee, [1939]. 272 pages. Illustrated by John R. Neill. First edition:

Textual points: 16-page gatherings. Pictorial endpapers in black and white. The front is a self-endpaper; the rear is inserted.

Cover: (Plate 88) various colors of cloth: vermilion, dark drab-green, beige (textured), tan, yellow-orange (textured and untextured), turquoise, brick-red, and bright medium blue have been reported. No priority is known. Pictorial paper label in colors. Spine imprint in semi-script, "fancy" letters.

Size of leaf: 9 by 6 5/8 inches. *Thickness of volume*: 1 1/4 inches.

Later Printings

Later printings have 32-page gatherings except for the penultimate (16 pages) and the last (8 pages); self-endpapers front and back.

ADDENDA — RUTH PLUMLY THOMPSON

In 1939, Ruth Plumly Thompson retired as Royal Historian of Oz. Thirty-three years (and seven Oz books by other authors) went by before her twentieth Oz title, *Yankee in Oz*, was published in 1972. Shortly before her death in 1976, Thompson added Oz elements to a previously unpublished story, *The Enchanted Island*, and it was published as *The Enchanted Island of Oz*.*

YANKEE IN OZ

Yankee in Oz. [Kinderhook, Illinois]: The International Wizard of Oz Club, Inc., [1972]. 94 pages. Illustrated by Dick Martin. Maps by James E. Haff. First edition, two printings:

1. *Textual points*: Bound in a single gathering, saddle wire-stitched (stapled in the center). Page [6] contains the copyright notice and an advertisement for *Animal Fairy Tales* and *Yankee in Oz*. Page [7] has a letter from the author with an address in Malvern, Pennsylvania, on the bottom left; there is a misprint in the final paragraph of the letter, "V" for "IV". Page [10] has the seal of The International Wizard of Oz Club. Page [12] has a picture of the Red Jinn twirling a parasol. The book ends with page [96], a blank verso. There are no endpapers.

Cover: (Plate 89) pictorial paper wrappers, trimmed to page size, printed on the front and back in color.

*Ruth Plumly Thompson's posthumous collection of primarily non-Oz stories and verses, *The Wizard of Way-Up and Other Wonders* (The International Wizard of Oz Club, 1985), contains two poems and one story about Oz.

SECONDARY BINDINGS: A few months after the publication of the paperbound state, about one hundred copies were bound in light-blue cloth with a pictorial paper label on the front (plate 90). The spine and back cover are blank. The book is side-stitched, and the paper wrappers are bound in as a double frontispiece. Still later, another fifty copies were bound in dark-gray cloth, with the same label. The label is narrow (10 1/4 by 3 inches), printed in black on yellow stock. About six labels were printed in black on red stock.

Size of leaf: 11 by 8 1/2 inches. *Thickness of volume:* A scant 1/4 inch. The copies in cloth are trimmed so that the size of the leaf is 10 3/4 by 8 1/4 inches; the thickness of volume is about 1/2 inch.

2. The second printing was published in two forms.

A) *Textual points:* "Perfect-bound," that is, the book is made up of single leaves held together at the spine with glue. The book reproduces on pages [2]-[3] the cover design of the first printing, in black and white. Including this picture required rearranging the preliminary and concluding material. The following are the most important changes. Page [8] contains the copyright notice followed by "First published 1972·Reprinted 1986 | Cover copyright 1986"; the seal of The International Wizard of Oz Club replaces the advertisement that appeared on the copyright page in the first printing. Page [9] has the letter from the author with an address in Berwyn, Pennsylvania, on the bottom left, and the misprint has been corrected. The picture of the Red Jinn twirling a parasol has been moved to page [96]. Pages [97]-[99] contain a list of nineteen "Special Publications" of The International Wizard of Oz Club, dated Autumn 1986. At the foot of page [99] is a printer's imprint of three lines. Page [100] has a picture of Yankee that was not in the first printing. There are no endpapers.

Cover: (Plate 91) pictorial stiff-paper wrappers, trimmed to page size, and printed on the front and back with new illustrations in color. The spine is blank.

B) *Textual points:* 16-page gatherings except for the final which contains 20 pages. Blank inserted endpapers. Otherwise the text is identical with A.

Cover: (Plate 92) gray-green cloth, stamped in black on the front with a reduced version of the drawing which was used as the front cover label of the first printing, secondary binding. The spine and the back cover are blank. Issued in a full-color dust jacket with illustrations and lettering identical with the wrappers of A. The front flap contains material about the story; the back flap lists 44 Oz books, followed by a picture of the Nome King.

THE ENCHANTED ISLAND OF OZ

The Enchanted Island of Oz. [Kinderhook, Illinois]: The International Wizard of Oz Club, Inc., [1976]. 77 pages. Illustrated by Dick Martin. Maps by James E. Haff. First edition:

Textual points: "Perfect-bound," that is, the book is made up of single leaves held together at the spine with glue. Page [79] contains a list of ten "Special Publications" of The International Wizard of Oz Club, dated Winter 1976. Issued with a loosely inserted errata sheet (4 by 8 1/4 inches) with a reduced reproduction of the illustration on page 56.

Cover: (Plate 93) pictorial stiff-paper wrappers, trimmed to page size, and printed on the front and back in color. The spine is blank.

Size of leaf: 11 by 8 1/2 inches. *Thickness of volume:* 1/4 inch.

There has been only one printing of this book.

THE OZ BOOKS OF JOHN R. NEILL

When Ruth Plumly Thompson left (temporarily) the Land of Oz, Reilly & Lee chose as her successor John R. Neill, the man who had illustrated the Oz books since 1904.

XXXIV. THE WONDER CITY OF OZ

The Wonder City of Oz. Chicago: Reilly & Lee, [1940]. 318 pages. Illustrated by John R. Neill. First edition:

Textual points: 16-page gatherings. Pictorial self-endpapers in black and white. The running-titles on pages 306-318 have the chapter-number on the versos (left-hand pages) and the book-title on the rectos (right-hand pages). The double-page picture on pages [292]-[293] is printed correctly.

Cover: (Plate 94) various colors of cloth: blue (textured and untextured), emerald-green (textured), light-green, red, very light beige, and orange (textured and untextured) have been reported. No priority is known. Pictorial paper label in colors. Spine imprint is in semi-script, "fancy" letters.

Size of leaf: 8 7/8 by 6 5/8 inches. *Thickness of volume*: 1 3/8 inches.

Later Printings

Later printings are made up of 32-page gatherings. The running-titles on pages 306-318 have the chapter-number on the rectos and the book-title on the versos. In re-imposing the book, the printer erroneously placed what had been the right section of the double-page picture onto page [292] and the left section onto page [293].

XXXV. THE SCALAWAGONS OF OZ

The Scalawagons of Oz. Chicago: Reilly & Lee, [1941]. 309 pages. Illustrated by John R. Neill. First edition:

Textual points: 16-page gatherings. Pictorial self-endpapers in black and white.

Cover: (Plate 95) various colors of cloth: copies have been reported in dark brick-red, very light brick-red, dark-red, rose, light gray-green, and dull-blue cloth. No priority is known. Pictorial paper label in colors. The title on the spine is printed diagonally, with the word "SCALA-WAGONS" hyphenated and on two lines with the word "OZ" printed as a stylized device, the "Z" within the "O". Spine imprint is in semi-script, "fancy" letters. The dust jacket has a misprint in the list of titles on the back flap, "Scallywagons" for "Scalawagons".

Size of leaf: 8 7/8 inches by 6 5/8 inches. *Thickness of volume*: 1 3/8 inches.

Later Printings

Later printings are made up of 32-page gatherings and have the word "SCALAWAGONS" on the spine printed diagonally, unhyphenated, on a single line and the word "OZ" printed not as a stylized device but as a conventional word (plate 96).

A dust jacket for a British issue of *The Scalawagons of Oz* is known. It is adapted from Neill's original design and contains the spine imprint of Hutchinson's Books for Young People. This jacket is probably a ca. 1945 proof for a projected but never-published volume.

XXXVI. LUCKY BUCKY IN OZ

Lucky Bucky in Oz. Chicago: Reilly & Lee, [1942]. 289
pages. Illustrated by John R. Neill. First edition:

Textual points: 16-page gatherings. Inserted pictorial endpapers.

Cover: (Plate 97) various colors of cloth: tan, turquoise, light
tannish-green, dark green, light green (textured and
untextured), light gray, sky-blue, bright blue, orange,
light orange-tan, yellow, and red have been reported. No
priority is known. Pictorial paper label in colors. The
spine title is printed in plain, unserifed letters, with the
word "OZ" as a stylized device, the "Z" within the "O".
The publisher's imprint on the spine is in the semi-script,
"fancy" letters. The jacket on the first state does not have
the usual list of Oz books on the back flap; instead, it has a
letter from "Bucky of Oz" asking readers to buy Victory
Bonds and Stamps.

Size of leaf: 8 7/8 by 6 5/8 inches. *Thickness of volume*:
1 3/8 inches.

Later Printings

Several copies have been seen printed on thinner stock,
measuring only one inch thick. They have 16-page gatherings
and blank endpapers. All the printing on the spine is plain,
unserifed square-cut capital letters with the "OZ" printed as
a word in conventional style rather than as a device. This
early printing, ca. 1944-1946, is bound in light-tan cloth.

All subsequent printings are made up of 32-page gatherings
and have the spine printing as on the first state described
above. The earlier of these have pictorial endpapers; later
copies have blank endpapers.

A British edition was published by Hutchinson's Books
for Young People (London). It is a larger book: size of leaf is
9 3/4 by 7 5/8 inches. The type has been completely reset and

some of the illustrations omitted, with the result that the book contains only 128 pages. Chapter 14 has been retitled from "Tea and Thunderbugs" to "Tea and Thunderbeetles" (and all references in chapters 14 and 15 altered accordingly) in keeping with modern British usage which does not recognize "bug" as a synonym for "insect." The endpapers of the American edition are replaced by reproductions of two of the double-page illustrations. The cover is red cloth, without a pictorial label (plate 98). The book is undated but was published in 1945.

ADDENDUM—JOHN R. NEILL

In 1915, without L. Frank Baum's approval, Reilly & Britton published *The Oz Toy Book*, a collection of cut-outs of the Oz characters designed by John R. Neill. The book was published primarily as an advertising gimmick.

THE OZ TOY BOOK

The Oz Toy Book, Cut-outs for the Kiddies. Chicago: The Reilly & Britton Co., [1915]. Illustrated by John R. Neill. 16 unnumbered leaves. First edition:

Textual points and *cover*: The book consists of 16 leaves plus front and back covers, all printed on thin bristol board. The leaves are printed in full color on rectos only; the versos are blank. The front cover (plate 99) is printed in full color; the verso contains instructions for cutting out the figures and making easels for standing them up. The back cover is blank; the recto contains a list of the Baum Oz books in which the various characters appear. The book is not bound in the technical sense: the leaves are separate and are tied together within the covers by string through perforations at the top and bottom left-hand corners. The covers are fastened together by a green-cloth spine.

Size of leaf: 8 1/4 by 11 1/4 inches. *Thickness of volume*: 1/4 inch.

Later Printings

A reprint without publisher's imprint or date was published in 1971 by The International Wizard of Oz Club. It contains reproductions of the original drawings in black and white; page numerals have been added. The pages are wire side-stitched (stapled) in stiff paper covers of peach-colored stock. The back cover is blank; the front cover, which reproduces the original cover design, is printed in black. The size of leaf is 8 1/2 by 11 inches. A second printing, also without publisher's imprint or date, was published in 1986 by The International Wizard of Oz Club. It is similar to the earlier reprint, but with an additional leaf containing an introduction by Barbara S. Koelle. The stiff wrappers are of white stock; the front reproduces the original cover design in color.

THE OZ BOOKS OF JACK SNOW

After John R. Neill's death in 1943, the high cost of book manufacturing and, it seems, a slowdown in sales of Oz books led to a delay in reviving the series. The publishers eventually chose as Royal Historian Jack Snow, a long-time writer for the radio and one of the first experts on L. Frank Baum. His two Oz stories were conscious attempts to recapture the feeling and even the language of Baum's Oz.

XXXVII. THE MAGICAL MIMICS IN OZ

The Magical Mimics in Oz. Chicago: The Reilly & Lee Co., [1946]. 242 pages. Illustrated by Frank Kramer. First edition:

Textual points: 16-page gatherings. The text is printed on white stock. Inserted pictorial endpapers printed in green on pale-yellow stock.

Cover: (Plate 100) light-gray cloth, with a pictorial paper label in colors. Spine imprint is in semi-script, "fancy" letters. The dust jacket has, instead of a list of Oz books on the back flap, a long statement about Jack Snow, Frank Kramer, and Baum's literary importance.

Size of leaf: 8 7/8 by 6 5/8 inches. *Thickness of volume*: Varies from 1 1/16 to 1 3/16 inches (text sheets including the free endpapers measure 15/16 to 1 1/16 inches thick from copy to copy). The height of the cover varies from 9 1/8 to 9 1/4 inches. (Copies have been seen bound in orange and in blue cloth, with the cover only 9 1/16 inches tall; they are probably later, perhaps around 1951.)

NOTE: Why first-printing copies vary in thickness is indicated by an inscription from publisher to author in an unbound, advance copy of *The Magical Mimics in Oz*: "Jack, Thought you would like to have this No. 1 — *Mimics* —even though this particular book does have two weights of paper—through press room error." This copy is exactly 1 inch thick without covers. Both paper stocks are white.

Later Printings

All subsequent printings retain the 16-page gatherings, but they are printed on a light-gray stock which is thinner than the white stocks used on the first state: the volume is only 7/8 inch thick. Earlier reprints retain the pictorial label and the illustrated endpapers.

In 1950, a "Popular Edition" appeared. It is printed on the light-gray paper stock and bound in light-brown paper-covered boards stamped in dark brown; there is no pictorial label (plate 101). The illustrated endpapers have been omitted, and the first page of the first gathering and the last page of the final gathering are pasted to the covers.

XXXVIII. THE SHAGGY MAN OF OZ

The Shaggy Man of Oz. Chicago: The Reilly & Lee Co., [1949]. 254 pages. Illustrated by Frank Kramer. First edition:

Textual points: 32-page gatherings. Inserted pictorial endpapers in black and white.

Cover: (Plate 102) gray cloth with a green cast. A few copies have been seen bound in light-gray cloth with a blue cast. Pictorial paper label in colors. Spine imprint is in semi-script, "fancy" letters.

Size of leaf: 8 7/8 by 6 1/2 inches. *Thickness of volume*: 1 1/8 inches.

Size of leaf: 8 7/8 by 6 1/2 inches. *Thickness of volume:*
1 1/8 inches.

Later Printings

Later printings have blank endpapers. The earlier of
these retain the pictorial paper label.

ADDENDUM—JACK SNOW

Jack Snow's last contribution to the Oz saga was *Who's Who in Oz*, a sort of Biographia Oziana containing informal biographies of the approximately six hundred characters in the first thirty-nine books in the regular Oz series.

WHO'S WHO IN OZ

Who's Who in Oz. Chicago: The Reilly & Lee Co., [1954]. 277 pages. Illustrated with reproductions of Oz illustrations by John R. Neill, Frank Kramer, and "Dirk" [Dirk Gringhuis]. First edition:

Textual points: 32-page gatherings. Inserted pictorial endpapers printed in brown on off-white stock.*

Cover: (Plate 103) tan cloth, stamped in brown and gilt; there is no pictorial paper label. The dust-jacket design differs from the cover design (plate 104).

Size of leaf: 8 7/8 by 6 5/8 inches. *Thickness of volume*: About 1 inch.

There has been only one printing of this book.

_____

*The endpaper design, a map of Oz and surrounding countries, was reprinted, ca. 1954, in reduced size in brown on tan card-stock. The back is blank.

THE OZ BOOK OF RACHEL R. COSGROVE

Rachel R. Cosgrove (now Rachel C. Payes) submitted to Reilly & Lee in 1950 the manuscript of an Oz story. The publisher accepted the manuscript, which was published the next year as the thirty-ninth book in the series. Among Mrs. Payes' later fiction are a detective novel and several gothic romances.

XXXIX. THE HIDDEN VALLEY OF OZ

The Hidden Valley of Oz. Chicago: The Reilly & Lee Co., [1951]. 313 pages. Illustrated by "Dirk" [Dirk Gringhuis]. First edition:

Textual points: 32-page gatherings. Pictorial self-endpapers in black and white.

Cover: (Plate 105) medium-blue cloth, with pictorial paper label in colors. Spine imprint is in semi-script, "fancy" letters.

Size of leaf: 8 3/4 by 6 3/8 inches. *Thickness of volume*: 1 3/8 inches. The volume is about 9 1/16 inches tall.

Later Printings

Later printings lack the pictorial label and are considerably taller (9 3/8 inches) and thinner (1 inch). Copies have been noted bound in yellow, blue, green, and light-red cloth. Some have pictorial endpapers; others have blank endpapers.

THE OZ BOOKS OF ELOISE JARVIS McGRAW AND LAUREN McGRAW WAGNER

During the 1950s, sales of the Oz books indicated to Reilly & Lee that the series had become top-heavy, that there was not a large enough market to make profitable any further expansion of the series. The purchase of the firm in 1959 by the Henry Regnery Company signalled a revival in interest in Oz-related publications. Reilly & Lee published *The Visitors from Oz; To Please a Child, a Biography of L. Frank Baum;* a series of Oz abridgments (see below, pp. 135-136); and *Merry Go Round in Oz* by Eloise Jarvis McGraw and her daughter Lauren McGraw Wagner. Mrs. McGraw has written many other children's books, including two runners-up for the Newbery Medal.

XL. MERRY GO ROUND IN OZ

Merry Go Round in Oz. Chicago: Reilly & Lee, [1963]. 303 pages. Illustrated by Dick Martin. First edition:

Textual points: 16-page gatherings. Inserted pictorial end-papers printed in brown on yellow stock.

Cover: (Plate 106) white cloth, printed in full color on the front, back, and spine. The drawing on the front cover is about 9 1/4 inches high. Head and tail-bands of blue-and-white striped fabric. The spine is hand-lettered, the imprint reads: "Reilly │ & Lee". Earliest copies distributed had a dust jacket printed in full color with the same design as that of the cover. Rather than the usual list of Oz books, the back flap contains comments about and photographs of the authors.

SECONDARY BINDING: White cloth. The front cover has a reproduction of the original front cover design in full color; the drawing has been reduced to about 7 3/4 inches. The back cover drawing is replaced by an overall criss-cross ruled design in tan. The spine-lettering is typeset. This casing was produced in the same way as secondary binding A of *The Visitors from Oz* (see above, p.81).

Size of leaf: 9 1/16 by 6 3/4 inches. *Thickness of volume*: 1 1/8 inches.

There has been only one printing of this book.

ADDENDUM— ELOISE JARVIS McGRAW AND LAUREN LYNN McGRAW

The Reilly & Lee Company published no new Oz books after *Merry Go Round in Oz*, but the firm gave the International Wizard of Oz Club permission to issue two additional Oz books by Ruth Plumly Thompson (described above, pp. 105-107) as well as a new tale of Oz by Eloise Jarvis McGraw and her daughter, who now uses her maiden name, Lauren Lynn McGraw.

THE FORBIDDEN FOUNTAIN OF OZ

The Forbidden Fountain of Oz. [Kinderhook, Illinois]: The International Wizard of Oz Club, Inc., [1980]. 98 pages. Illustrated by Dick Martin. First edition:

Textual points: "Perfect-bound," that is, the book is made up of single leaves held together at the spine with glue. Pages [101]-[102] contain a list of eleven "Special Publications" of The International Wizard of Oz Club, dated Spring 1980. At the foot of page [102] is a printer's imprint of three lines.

Cover: (Plate 107) pictorial stiff-paper wrappers, trimmed to page size, and printed on the front and back in color. The spine is blank.

Size of leaf: 10 15/16 by 8 7/16 inches. *Thickness of volume*: 5/16 inch.

There has been only one printing of this book.

121

THE OZ BOOK OF DICK MARTIN

In addition to illustrating a number of full-length Oz books, Dick Martin has designed many Oz-related publications, including a set of Oz maps, a collection of his Oz drawings under the title *An Oz Picture Gallery*, and cut-out books of Oz masks, of the Emerald City, and of an Oz theater. He has now become the most recent of Reilly & Lee Oz authors or illustrators to write a chronicle of Oz.

THE OZMAPOLITAN OF OZ

The Ozmapolitan of Oz. [Kinderhook, Illinois]: The International Wizard of Oz Club, Inc., [1986]. 101 pages. Illustrated by Dick Martin. First edition, published in two forms:

A) *Textual points*: "Perfect-bound," that is, the book is made up of single leaves held together at the spine with glue. Pages [103]-[104] contain a list of eighteen "Special Publications" of The International Wizard of Oz Club, dated Spring 1986. At the foot of page [104] is a printer's imprint of three lines. There are no endpapers.

Cover: (Plate 108). Pictorial laminated stiff-paper wrappers trimmed to page size, and printed on the front and back in color. The spine is blank.

Size of leaf: 10 15/16 by 8 7/16 inches. *Thickness of volume*: 5/16 inch.

B) *Textual points*: 16-page gatherings, except for the penultimate which contains 24 pages. Blank inserted endpapers. Most copies have all pages integral, but some were damaged in the binding process, resulting in the insertion of 4-page conjugate cancels at any or all of the following places: pages 15-18, [31]-34, 47-[50], 87-90.

Cover: (Plate 109) red cloth, stamped on the front in black. The spine and the back cover are blank. Issued in a full-color dust jacket with illustrations and lettering identical with the wrappers of A. The front and back flaps are blank.

Size of leaf: 11 by 8 7/16 inches. *Thickness of volume:* 1/2 inch.

There has been only one printing of this book.

CURIOSA

W.W. DENSLOW

W.W. Denslow's illustrations had contributed considerably to the success of *The Wonderful Wizard of Oz* as a book and as a musical extravaganza. As co-owner of the copyright of the first Oz book, he felt within his rights to prepare books using the Oz characters. *Pictures from The Wonderful Wizard of Oz* uses the color plates from the Geo. M. Hill edition, but the story printed with them in this pamphlet has nothing to do with Oz. *Denslow's Scarecrow and the Tin-Man* is about those two characters as actors in the musical extravaganza rather than as residents of Oz. Denslow also wrote and illustrated a series of newspaper stories about the Scarecrow and the Tin Woodman; these tales begin in Oz but quickly come to our world.*

PICTURES FROM THE WONDERFUL WIZARD OF OZ

Pictures from The Wonderful Wizard of Oz. Chicago: George W. Ogilvie & Co., n.d., [ca. 1903-1904]. 42 pages. Story by Thomas H. Russell. Illustrations by W.W. Denslow. First edition:

Textual points and *color plates*: The book is made up of the Geo. M. Hill color-plate sheets from *The Wonderful Wizard of Oz*. All 24 plates are included, but two of them are pasted down on the front and back covers and only the blank versos are visible. On the backs of the plates

*For further information on Denslow bibliography, see *W.W. Denslow* (Clark Historical Library, Central Michigan University, 1976) by Douglas G. Greene and Michael Patrick Hearn and "A Bibliography of the Work of W.W. Denslow: Additions and Corrections," also by Hearn and Greene (*The Baum Bugle*, Autumn 1980).

appears Russell's story. Bound as a single gathering, saddle wire-stitched (stapled in the center).

Cover: (Plate 110) stiff paper wrappers, printed in colors. The spine has been seen in green, dark-red, or brown cloth. The illustrations on the front and back covers are not by Denslow.

Size of leaf: 8 1/4 by 6 1/2 inches. *Thickness of volume:* 1/8 inch.

There was apparently only one printing of the entire booklet, although the cover and story were included in *The Annotated Wizard of Oz*, edited by Michael Patrick Hearn (Clarkson N. Potter, 1973).

DENSLOW'S SCARECROW AND THE TIN-MAN

Denslow's Scarecrow and The Tin-Man. New York: G.W. Dillingham Co., [1904]. 12 unnumbered pages. Written and illustrated by W.W. Denslow. First edition, two states:

1. *Textual points:* Published both on stiff paper and on paper mounted on linen. The paper-stock is pebbled. Textual illustrations in color. Bound in single gathering, saddle wire-stitched (stapled in the center).

Cover: (Plate 111) stiff paper or paper mounted on linen; printed in colors on front and back. The back cover has an advertisement for *Denslow's New Series of Picture Books,* 1904.

Size of leaf: 11 by 8 3/8 inches. *Thickness of volume:* Approximately 1/16 inch (on stiff paper); approximately 1/8 inch (on paper mounted on linen).

2. *Textual points* and *cover:* Same as #1 except that the pamphlet is printed on smooth paper-stock, and that there

is a printer's imprint for the J.J. Little Company at the foot of the inside back cover.

Later Printings

Around 1913, *Denslow's Scarecrow and The Tin-Man* was reprinted as a pamphlet by M.A. Donohue & Co. of Chicago. It is similar to the earlier states with the following exceptions: the Donohue imprint replaces Dillingham on the cover; the back cover has a reproduction of the picture on page [11]; and the pamphlet has larger dimensions. The page size of some copies is 11 1/4 by 9 inches; of others, it is 11 1/2 by 9 3/8 inches.

The story appeared in *Five Favorite Stories*, published by The American Crayon Company in 1943, with redrawings of some of the Denslow illustrations. When this collection was reprinted in 1946, the cover title was changed to *More than Five Favorite Stories*. Also in 1946, The American Crayon Company published the story with the same illustrations in *More than 30 of American Childhood's Best Books*.

Scarecrow and Tin-Man (with a slight change in title) was printed as a pamphlet by Perks Publishing in 1946 (plate 112), with redrawings of the illustrations by "Mary and Wallace Stover after Denslow." The pamphlet also contains "Slovenly Peter" and a few other pieces not by Denslow. There are two states. What is probably the earlier gives New York as the place of publication, and the pictures are printed in black and yellow. What is probably the later gives Silver Spring, Maryland, as the place of publication, and the pictures are printed in alternating spreads of black and blue, and black and yellow.

The Annotated Wizard of Oz (1973) reproduces, in much reduced size, the first edition, second state of *Denslow's Scarecrow and The Tin-Man*.

DENSLOW'S SCARECROW AND THE TIN-MAN AND OTHER STORIES

This volume is a clothbound collection containing *Denslow's Scarecrow and The Tin-Man* and the other five Denslow picture books issued by Dillingham in 1904.

Denslow's Scarecrow and The Tin-Man and Other Stories. New York: G.W. Dillingham Co., [1904]. 74 unnumbered pages. Written and illustrated by W.W. Denslow. First edition:

Textual points: Textual illustrations in color. Inserted pictorial endpapers printed in blue and orange on off-white stock; on the front paste-down is the imprint: "Press of J.J. Little & Co. | Astor Place, New York". One copy, probably a binder's error, has been seen with blank enpapers.

Cover: (Plate 113) light-green cloth, stamped in brown. A small picture of the Scarecrow's head appears in the upper right-hand corner of the front cover, and within a stamped frame at the lower left is a pictorial paper label in colors. The title, "Denslow's SCARECROW AND THE TIN-MAN" is stamped in brown on the spine vertically from top to bottom.

Size of leaf: 11 by 8 7/16 inches. *Thickness of volume:* About 1/2 inch.

A British issue was received at the Bodleian Library on September 14, 1904. It is identical with the American edition except that the title page is a cancel with the imprint of T. Fisher Unwin of London.

Later Printings

Around 1913, *Denslow's Scarecrow and The Tin-Man and Other Stories* was reprinted by M.A. Donohue & Co., of Chicago.

Textual points: The text is the same as that of the first state. Earlier Donohue copies have inserted pictorial endpapers printed in blue and yellow and a cancel title page with the Donohue imprint. Later copies have integral title pages. Some of these copies have blank self-endpapers in front and blank inserted endpapers in back; other copies have blank self-endpapers in front and the last sheet of the terminal gathering pasted to the back cover.

Cover: Various colors of cloth stamped in black. The Donohue cover is similar to that of the first edition, but the lettering on the front and spine has been reset, the Scarecrow's head has been deleted, and the title on the spine does not contain "Denslow's".

FRANK [JOSLYN] BAUM

Frank Joslyn Baum, L. Frank Baum's eldest son, wanted to continue the Oz series, but at his father's death he was in the American Expeditionary Force in France, and by the time he returned to the United States, Ruth Plumly Thompson had become Royal Historian of Oz. He wrote a full-length fantasy, *Rosine in Oz*, but Reilly & Lee declined to publish it. In 1932, he arranged with David Graham Fischer, Publisher, of Hollywood to issue the story as *Rosine and the Laughing Dragon*, but all that survives of that project is a single proof for the dust jacket or, possibly, the cover design. Two years later, Frank J. Baum reached an agreement with the Whitman Publishing Company to publish a portion of the manuscript as *The Laughing Dragon of Oz*. To prepare his ground for the legal case that Reilly & Lee was certain to bring, he registered the word "OZ" as a trademark and, around April 1934, printed a pamphlet of 8 pages, *Jimmy Bulber of Oz*, to show that he was using the trademark. (The story was reprinted in *Oziana* 4, 1974.) In January 1935, Whitman published *The Laughing Dragon of Oz* as Big Little Book number 1126. Publisher and author planned a sequel to be entitled *The Enchanted Princess of*

Oz. Reportedly the second book was in proofs when Reilly & Lee brought suit. The matter was settled in 1936 when Whitman agreed not to publish *The Enchanted Princess of Oz* or to reprint *The Laughing Dragon of Oz*. Reilly & Lee also claimed that "OZ" was its common-law trademark, and won that point in a separate case.

THE LAUGHING DRAGON OF OZ

The Laughing Dragon of Oz. Racine, Wisconsin: Whitman Publishing Co., [1934].* 425 pages. Illustrated by Milt Youngren. First edition:

Textual points: "Perfect-bound," that is, the book is made up of single leaves held together at the spine with glue. There are no color plates, but approximately every other page is a full-page, black-and-white picture. There are three pages of advertisements at the end of the book.

Cover: (Plate 114) pictorial paper-covered boards, printed on the front, back, and spine in colors.

Size of leaf: 4 1/8 by 3 7/16 inches. *Thickness of volume*: 1 1/2 inches.

ALEXANDER VOLKOV

In recent years, pastiches and other extensions or reinterpretations of the Oz saga have abounded. These publications include Oz books written by enthusiasts and usually published privately (Henry Blossom's *The Blue Emperor of Oz*, Chris Dulabone's *Toto in Oz*, March Laumer's *The Green Dolphin of Oz* and *Aunt Em and Uncle Henry in Oz*, Onyx Madden's *The Mysterious Chronicles of Oz*, Harry Mongold's *The Sawhorse of Oz* and *Button Bright of Oz*, Hugh Pendexter III's *Oz and the Three Witches* and Ray

*Although copyrighted 1934, the book was not published until January 1935.

Powell's *Mr. Flint in Oz*), commercially published books and booklets (Philip Jose Farmers's *A Barnstormer in Oz*, Polly Berends's *Ozma and the Wayward Wand*, James Howe's *Mr. Tinker in Oz*, Susan Saunders's *Dorothy and the Magic Belt*, and Dorothy Haas's *Dorothy and the Seven-Leaf Clover* and *Dorothy and Old King Crow*), a parody (the title story in Dave Morrah's *Der Wizard in Ozzenland)*, graphic novels (Eric Shanower's *The Enchanted Apples of Oz* and *The Secret Island of Oz*), retellings of movies and television shows (Joan Vinge's *Return to Oz* and Romeo Muller's *Dorothy and the Green Gobbler of Oz*), and a so-called "healthier" version of the first Oz book (Richard Gardner's *Dorothy and the Lizard of Oz*). Many of these books are interesting, but they are peripheral to the purpose of *Bibliographia Oziana*.

A more independent development, yet one that indicates the growing influence of L. Frank Baum's creation, is the series of books by the Russian author Alexander Volkov (1890-1976). In 1939, Volkov wrote a Russian adaptation of *The Wizard of Oz* under the title *Volsebnik Izumrudnogo Goroda* ("The Wizard of the Emerald City" — the word "Oz" is not mentioned in the book). Although Volkov is credited with the authorship, and the names of the main characters are changed to Ellie, Totoshka, the Iron Woodchopper, and the Strawman, the book is basically a retelling of Baum's story with the addition of some subplots. After the success of a revised version in 1959, Volkov followed with a series of his own novels about the Oz characters: *Urfin Dzjus i ego Derevjannye Soldaty* ("Urfin Dzjus and His Wooden Soldiers," 1963), *Sem' Podzemnyh Korolej* ("Seven Underground Kings," 1969), *Ognennyj Bog Marranov* ("The Fire God of the Maronnes," 1972), *Zeltyj Tuman* ("The Yellow Fog," 1974), *Zabrosynnovo Zamka* ("The Secret of the Deserted Castle," 1982). Two of these sequels have been published in English. Both books are free translations, restoring Baum's names to the characters and calling Volkov's fairyland "Oz."

THE WOODEN SOLDIERS OF OZ

The Wooden Soldiers of Oz. Hong Kong: Opium Books, 1969. [x] + 266 pages. Translated from the Russian by Mary G. Langford. Illustrated by L. Vladimirskov (adapted by Lau Shiu Fan). Decorations by Michael Patrick Hearn. Introduction by Douglas and David Greene. First edition:

Textual points: 32-page gatherings except for a terminal gathering of 24 pages. Printed in two colors, slate green and burgundy red. The bottom of the pages is deckle-edged, and some of the copies were issued with the pages "unopened" at the bottom, that is, the bottoms of the leaves were still attached to one another. Inserted pictorial endpapers printed in slate green. At the foot of the recto of the rear free endpaper is a printer's imprint of one line.

Cover: (Plate 115) pictorial stiff paper-wrappers, trimmed to page size, and printed on the front, back, and spine in colors.

Size of leaf: 7 7/16 by 5 1/4 inches. *Thickness of volume*: approximately 3/4 inch.

There has been only one printing of this book.

YELLOW FOG OVER OZ

Yellow Fog Over Oz. [Albuquerque: Buckethead Enterprises of Oz, 1986.] [iv] + 232 pages. Translated from the Russian by March Laumer. [Illustrated by Chris Dulabone.] First edition:

Textual points: "Perfect-bound," that is, the book is made up of single leaves held together at the spine with glue. Printed on yellow paper-stock. The verso of the title page contains notices that "this edition" (i.e. the translation) is copyrighted 1983, and that the illustrations are copyrighted 1986. Following the second copyright notice is: *"First printing in this edition:* | *October 1986* | *printed by*

THE QUIET PRESS". Pages 233-[234] are headed "EPILOZ" and announce future publications; the name of the publisher, Buckethead Enterprises of Oz, is given on these pages for the first time in the book. There are no endpapers.

Cover: (Plate 116) yellow stiff paper-wrappers, trimmed to page size, and lettered on the front and the spine in green. The back cover is blank.

Size of leaf: 8 5/16 by 5 3/8 inches. *Thickness of volume:* approximately 5/8 inch.

There has been only one printing of this book.

APPENDIX 1:
AUTHORIZED ADAPTATIONS
AND ABRIDGMENTS OF THE OZ BOOKS

1939 RAND McNALLY "JUNIOR EDITIONS"

In March 1939, probably to take advantage of the publicity surrounding the forthcoming MGM film of *The Wizard of Oz*, Rand McNally and Company issued three volumes containing the six *Little Wizard Stories* (see above, p. 84-85). Three months later, the company followed with the first abridgments of any of the Oz books other than *The Wizard of Oz*. The most notable volume in this series is the abridgment of *The Road to Oz*, the only edition of that story to contain any of Neill's illustrations in full color. (The pictures were, however, reworked by a staff artist, not by Neill himself.) The six abridgments and the three *Little Wizard* volumes were sold separately and as a complete set in a decorated box, *The Wonderful Land of Oz Library* (plate 117).

The Land of Oz, The Road to Oz, The Emerald City of Oz, The Patchwork Girl of Oz, Rinkitink in Oz, and *The Lost Princess of Oz*. Chicago: Rand McNally & Company, [1939]. 62 pages in each volume. Illustrated by John R. Neill.

Textual points: On the foot of the last page is "CS 6-39". The final leaf has advertisements on both the recto and the verso. There are no color plates but each volume contains twelve full-page textual illustrations in full-color. Wire side-stitched (stapled).

Cover: (Plates 118-119) pictorial paper-covered boards, printed in color. The front cover designs are reworkings of those on the Reilly & Lee editions of the late 1930s.

Size of leaf: 6 3/8 by 5 1/4 inches. *Thickness of each volume:* Approximately 1/4 inch.

Later Printings

Later printings have been noted with "CS 8-39" or "CS 10-39" on the foot of the last page. The final leaf in the latter contains advertisements only on the recto.

1951 AND 1952 LITTLE GOLDEN BOOK ADAPTATIONS

The three Little Golden Books omit so much from the original stories that they are adapted rather than abridged versions. *The Road to Oz* contains brief retellings of only the Foxville, Johnny Dooit, and birthday-party episodes. *The Emerald City of Oz* has nothing about the Nome King and his attempt to conquer Oz. *The Tin Woodman of Oz* does not mention Woot or the Tin Soldier, and concentrates on the adventures with Mrs. Yoop.

The Road to Oz, The Emerald City of Oz, and *The Tin Woodman of Oz.* New York: Simon and Schuster, [first book, 1951; other books, 1952]. 28 unnumbered pages in each volume. Adapted by Peter Archer. Illustrated by Harry McNaught.

Textual points: Wire side-stitched (stapled). Illustrated on every page, with some pictures in full color and others in black and red. Pictorial lining papers on the inside of the front and back covers. A small capital letter "A" is printed on the bottom right of page [28].

Cover: (Plates 120-122) pictorial paper-covered boards, trimmed to page size. The front has the title and an illustration in full color. The upper right has the number of the volume: "144" for *The Road to Oz,* "151" for *The Emerald City of Oz,* "159" for *The Tin Woodman of Oz.* The back cover contains a list of titles in "The Little Golden Library". The list was changed as books were omitted when they went out of stock, and re-listed as they were reprinted. The following are the earliest reported lists:

The Road to Oz: The numbers in the right-hand column end with "144" and then continue to "D23".

The Emerald City of Oz: The numbers in the right-hand column end with "205" and then continue to "D23".

The Tin Woodman of Oz: The numbers in the right-hand column end with "205" and then continue to "D30". There are variations in the titles included in the list, but no priority is known.

Size of leaf: approximately 8 by 6 1/8 inches (measured from the wire-stitching). *Thickness of each volume*: 7/32 inch.

Later Printings

Copies of *The Road to Oz* have been reported with "B" on page [28], and with lists ending with "205" and "D30". Copies of *The Emerald City of Oz*, still with "A" on page [28], have been reported with lists ending with "205" and "D30".

1961 REILLY & LEE ADAPTATIONS

This series contains the first newly illustrated editions of *Ozma of Oz* and *Dorothy and the Wizard in Oz*. The retellings are generally faithful to the original tales, but do not retain much of Baum's language and an episode was omitted from each volume: the trip to the south and the visit with Glinda from *The Wizard of Oz*, the Jackdaws' Nest from *The Land of Oz*, the meeting with Langwidere from *Ozma of Oz*, and the trial of Eureka from *Dorothy and the Wizard in Oz*.

The Wizard of Oz, The Land of Oz, Ozma of Oz, and *Dorothy and the Wizard in Oz*. Chicago: The Reilly & Lee Co., [1961]. 60 unnumbered pages in each volume. Adapted by Jean Kellogg. Illustrated by Dick Martin.

Textual points: Bound in a single gathering, sewn in the center, with the outer leaves serving as paste-down lining papers. Printed so that two pages with pictures in full color are followed by two pages with pictures in black and white, throughout each book. The first copies printed of *Dorothy and The Wizard in Oz* have the final word on page [21] cutting into the illustration; this error was discovered and corrected during the press-run. No textual variations have been discovered in the other volumes.

Cover: (Plates 123-126) pictorial, laminated paper-covered boards, printed on the front, back, and spine in full color.

SECONDARY BINDINGS: The four books occur in two different cloth bindings produced primarily for libraries, although B was also available for sale to the general public.

A) The front cover has a slightly reduced, full-color reproduction of the original front cover design. The back covers of *The Wizard of Oz* and *Ozma of Oz* have an overall criss-cross ruled design. The back covers of *The Land of Oz* and *Dorothy and the Wizard in Oz* are blank. These binding-cases were produced in the same way as secondary binding A of *The Visitors from Oz* (see above, p. 81).

B) The front cover has a silk-screened re-drawn version of a Dick Martin illustration. *The Wizard of Oz* adapts the illustration from page [21] showing Dorothy asleep in the poppy field; it is printed in black, white and orange. The back cover is blank except for the imprint of American Publishers Corporation.* *The Land of Oz* adapts the original front cover design, but prints the title at the top rather than at the bottom; it is printed in black, yellow, and red. The back cover is blank, with no imprint. *Ozma of Oz* adapts the original front cover design in

*Secondary binding B of *The Visitors from Oz*, however, has an imprint for American Publisher's *Company*, not *Corporation*.

black, white, and orange; the back cover is blank with no imprint. *Dorothy and the Wizard in Oz* adapts the original front cover design in black, white, and blue; the back cover is blank except for the imprint of American Publisher's Corporation.

Size of leaf: 11 11/16 by 8 5/8 inches. *Thickness of each volume:* 5/8 inch. Copies in the secondary bindings are normally thicker and the pages have been trimmed to a smaller size.

There was only one printing of each volume.

APPENDIX 2:
SOME LATER DUST-JACKET AND COVER
DESIGNS OF THE OZ SERIES

By the late 1950s, Reilly & Lee ceased using pictorial labels on the front covers of the Oz books, and introduced a series of changes to make the series more modern in appearance.

a) About 1959, eleven Oz titles were issued in new dust jackets (plates 127-128) designed by a commercial illustrating firm; they are signed "Roycraft": *The Wizard of Oz, The Land of Oz, Ozma of Oz, Dorothy and the Wizard in Oz, The Road to Oz, The Scarecrow of Oz, The Lost Princess of Oz, The Tin Woodman of Oz, The Hungry Tiger of Oz, Pirates in Oz,* and *Speedy in Oz.*

b) In 1960, ten books were issued in new dust jackets (plates 129-130) designed by Dick Martin: *The Wizard of Oz* (replacing the Roycraft design when that was out of stock), *The Patchwork Girl of Oz, Rinkitink in Oz, The Magic of Oz, Glinda of Oz, Kabumpo in Oz, The Cowardly Lion of Oz, The Purple Prince of Oz, Captain Salt in Oz,* and *The Shaggy Man of Oz.*

c) In 1964, Reilly & Lee launched a new series of L. Frank Baum's Oz titles, bound in substantial cloth with color illustrations imprinted directly on the cloth. Dick Martin designed each volume using original illustrations and related material by W.W Denslow and John R. Neill. For the new cover for the 1964 version of *The Wizard of Oz*, Martin adapted a 1900 Denslow poster as a wrap-around, full-color design, and he also chose Denslow's endpaper design from *The New Wizard of Oz* (1903) for the endpapers of the 1964 printing. For the cover of the 1964 printing of *Tik-Tok of Oz* (plate 131), he adapted a 1914 drawing by John R. Neill originally intended for but not used as a wrap-around dust jacket design for the first edition of that title. Except for the wrap-around full-color cover of the *Wizard*, the remainder of the covers for the new series had the color-printing and lettering imprinted on white background, and therefore are often called the "white-cover" printings. The endpapers for the titles after the *Wizard* in the series reproduced Neill's original endpapers for the first edition of *The Road to Oz*. Six titles were published in the new series in 1964 (all issued without dust jackets): *The Wizard of Oz, The Emerald City of Oz, The Patchwork Girl of Oz, Tik-Tok of Oz, The Scarecrow of Oz,* and *The Lost Princess of Oz.*

d) In 1965, Dick Martin replaced his earlier cover for *The Wizard of Oz* with a new design printed on white background to be uniform with the rest of the series. In designing the new version of *The Tin Woodman of Oz*, he reinstated Neill's original illustrations. The nine titles produced in 1965 were: *The Wizard of Oz* (replacing the 1964 cover design), *The Land of Oz* (plate 132), *Ozma of Oz, Dorothy and the Wizard in Oz, The Road to Oz, Rinkitink of Oz, The Tin Woodman of Oz, The Magic of Oz,* and *Glinda of Oz.*

e) From 1971 to 1973, Rand McNally issued paperback versions of the new Reilly & Lee Baum Oz books, using the cover designs produced by Dick Martin. The Rand McNally volumes measure approximately 9 1/4 by 6 3/8 inches. Rand McNally published only 12 of Baum's 14 titles, omitting *The Lost Princess of Oz* and *Rinkitink in Oz* from its series.

f) In 1976, Henry Regnery Company, the proprietor of the Reilly & Lee imprint at the time, introduced its own paperback series of Baum's Oz books, in the "Wonderful World of Oz Series." These volumes, too, used the covers designed by Dick Martin, but are in a format smaller than the Rand McNally series, measuring approximately 7 by 5 inches. Regnery published four titles in the paperback series in 1976: *The Wizard of Oz, Ozma of Oz, The Scarecrow of Oz,* and *Rinkitink in Oz.*

g) From 1977 to 1979, Contemporary Books, successors to the Henry Regnery Company, added several titles per year to the "Wonderful World of Oz Series," until all fourteen of Baum's titles were reprinted.

h) In 1979, Ballantine Books, through arrangement with Contemporary Books, began production of still another paperback series of Baum's Oz titles in its Del Rey line of fantasy novels (plates 133-134). The new volumes measure approximately 7 by 4 1/8 inches and each title has a new, full-color design reproducing an original painting by Michael Herring. By 1981, all fourteen of Baum's Oz books were available in the Del Rey series. The text of the volumes were completely reset, so they represent completely new editions. Original illustrations by Denslow and Neill were used to illustrate the volumes.

i) In 1985 and 1986, the Del Rey line was expanded by Ballantine to include the Oz books of Ruth Plumly Thompson from *The Royal Book of Oz* through *The Wishing Horse of Oz* (plates 135-136). The texts of the volumes were completely reset. Michael Herring also produced new original paintings for the covers of the Thompson titles. The Thompson volumes are taller than the Baum series, measuring approximately 8 by 4 1/2 inches.

OZ BOOKS

1. **The Enchanted Island of Oz** by Ruth Plumly Thompson. Illustrated by Dick Martin. David Perry in America is amazed when he wishes a circus camel can talk—and it can! Other wishes come true, too, and David and Humpty Bumpty the camel have one Oz experience after another. Eventually they find themselves on Kapurta, an island stranded in the sky. How David Perry supplies the magic to move the island and how they all visit the Emerald City in time for the Cowardly Lion's birthday party make a good Oz adventure. Price per copy $12.00 (paperbound). *An original publication of the International Wizard of Oz Club.*

2. **The Forbidden Fountain of Oz** by Eloise Jarvis McGraw and Lauren Lynn McGraw. Illustrated by Dick Martin. One swallow of the magic water from the Forbidden Fountain and Ozma forgets who she is and disappears so completely that not even the Magic Picture can tell where she is. Price per copy $12.00 (paperbound). *An original publication of the International Wizard of Oz Club.*

3. **Handy Mandy in Oz** by Ruth Plumly Thompson. Illustrated by John R. Neill. Price per copy $25.00 (clothbound, no jacket), $12.00 (paperbound)

4. **The Hidden Prince of Oz** by Gina Wickwar. Illustrated by Anna-Maria Cool. Published in celebration of the hundredth anniversary of L. Frank Baum's The Wonderful Wizard of Oz. When the Glass Cat of Oz attends the dedication of Silica Valley's Great Glass-works, she doesn't know she's about to find her roots and be wished smack dab into the middle of the one-hundred-and-one-year-old mystery of the Hidden Prince of Oz! Regular edition sold out, signed/numbered limited boxed edition 1/100 **still available** for $100.00 (clothbound). *An original publication of the International Wizard of Oz Club.*

5. **The Hidden Valley of Oz** by Rachel Cosgrove. Illustrated by Dirk. Jam, a boy from America, arrives in Oz to discover that the citizens of the Hidden Valley are oppressed by a wicked giant. He escapes from the giant and has adventures with an oversized rat, snowmen, bookmen, and magic kites. He meets Dorothy, the Scarecrow, the Tin Woodman, the Cowardly Lion, and

141

the Hungry Tiger. With these friends, Jam returns to the Hidden Valley and learns the secret of the giant. Price per copy $25.00 (clothbound), $12.00 (paperbound)

6. **The Magical Mimics In Oz** by Jack Snow. Illustrated by Frank Kramer. Price per copy $25.00 (clothbound), $12.00 (paperbound)

7. **The Ozmapolitan of Oz** written and illustrated by Dick Martin. Dorothy and Eureka have an astonishing Oz adventure while looking for the source of the Winkie River and the whereabouts of the Scarecrow and the Tin Woodman. Price per copy $25.00 (clothbound), $12.00 (paperbound). *An original publication of the International Wizard of Oz Club.*

8. **Ozoplaning with the Wizard of Oz** by Ruth Plumly Thompson. Illustrated by John R. Neill. Price per copy $25.00 (clothbound), $12.00 (paperbound)

9. **The Scarecrow of Oz** by L. Frank Baum. Illustrated by John R. Neill. This edition includes the original twelve color illustrations. Price per copy $30.00 (clothbound)

10. **The Shaggy Man of Oz** by Jack Snow. Illustrated by Frank Kramer. Price per copy $25.00 (clothbound), $12.00 (paperbound)

11. **The Silver Princess in Oz** by Ruth Plumly Thompson. Illustrated by John R. Neill. Price per copy $25.00 (clothbound), $12.00 (paperbound)

12. **Speedy in Oz** by Ruth Plumly Thompson. Illustrated by John R. Neill. This edition includes the original twelve color illustrations. Price per copy $30.00 (clothbound)

13. **The Wicked Witch of Oz** by Rachel Cosgrove Payes. Designed and illustrated by Eric Shanower. The second Oz book by the author of *The Hidden Valley of Oz* introduces us to Singra, the Wicked Witch of the South, who has awakened after a one-hundred-year nap. In a quest to catch up with all the evil she has missed out on, Singra plots against the denizens of the Emerald City. Price per copy $24.95 (clothbound). Signed/numbered limited boxed edition 1/200 $100.00 (leather bound). *An original publication of the International Wizard of Oz Club.*

14. **The Wishing Horse of Oz** by Ruth Plumly Thompson. Illustrated by John R. Neill. This edition includes the original twelve color illustrations. Price per copy $30.00 (clothbound)

SPECIAL PUBLICATIONS

15. **Yankee in Oz** by Ruth Plumly Thompson. Illustrated by Dick Martin. Maps by James E. Haff. Tompy, a drummer boy from the U.S.A. and Yankee, an Air Force dog meet the Red Jinn of Ev and together they defeat a wicked giant who is threatening America and Oz. Price per copy, $25.00 (clothbound, no jacket), $12.00 (paperbound). *An original publication of the International Wizard of Oz Club.*

OTHER PUBLICATIONS AND PRODUCTS

16. **Animal Fairy Tales** by L. Frank Baum. Illustrated by Dick Martin. Introduction by Russell P. MacFall. Nine stories about animals and their fairy guardians. 151 pp., 5-1/2 x 8. **SALE PRICE!** $5.00 (paperbound) and $10.00 (clothbound).

17. **Bibliographia Oziana** by Peter E. Hanff, Douglas G. Greene, et al. $25.00 (paperbound)

18. **Oz Club Annual Illustrated Calendars.** 1984, 1990, 1991, 1993-2002 available in limited quantities. Price $5.00 each.

19. **The Cheerful Citizens of Oz** by Ruth Plumly Thompson. Illustrated by Rob Roy MacVeigh. The Scarecrow, the Hungry Tiger, Tik-Tok, Kabumpo, the Wizard, and even the Soldier with the Green Whiskers are among the characters to have their own poems in this volume. Most are here for the first time. Price per copy $8.00 (paperbound)

20. **The Curious Cruise of Captain Santa** by Ruth Plumly Thompson. Illustrated by John R. Neill. Thompson and Neill's only non-Oz collaboration. Price per copy $12.00 (paperbound)

21. **The Index to The Baum Bugle** by Frederick E. Otto and Dick Rutter. This index covers The Baum Bugle from 1957–2001. This index newly revised and expanded by Dick Rutter is a great help in finding material in more than 90 Bugles! Price per copy $15.00 (paperbound)

22. **The Ozmapolitan Game** by Dick Martin. Playing cards featuring Oz characters along with directions for games. Price per set $8.00.

23. **Oziana** the annual magazine of original Oz stories and illustrations. Issues currently available in limited quantities: 1981, 1983, 1984, 1986, 1988 and 1989 at $6.00 each; 1990, 1993, 1994, 1997-2000 at $4.00 each; 2001 and 2002 at $5.00 each (with color covers).

SPECIAL PUBLICATIONS

24. **The Oz Game Book** edited by Robin Olderman. Illustrations by W. W. Denslow, John R. Neill, Dick Martin, Bill Eubank, and others. The challenging quizzes, perplexing puzzles, and fun games in this book will add a new dimension to the enjoyment of Oz. Price per copy $6.00 (paperbound)

25. **An Oz Picture Gallery** by Dick Martin. A book of original drawings of Oz characters. 36 pp., 8 ½ x 11." Price per copy $8.00.

26. **An Oz Sketchbook** by Dick Martin. A new glimpse of familiar Oz characters in this book of original drawings. 40 pp., 8 ½ x 11." Price per copy $8.00.

27. **The Oz Toy Book** by John R. Neill. Introduction by Barbara S. Koelle. This contains original illustrations of characters from the first nine Oz books. 16 pp. 8 ½ x 11." Price per copy $6.00 (paperbound).

28. **Set of Oz Maps** - $7.00 per set of two maps with explanatory leaflet.

29. **Oz map pin**, made of jeweler's metal and enameled in the Oz colors, made by the cloisonné process to assure permanent color. $15.00 per pin.

30. **Twinkle and Chubbins** by L. Frank Baum. Illustrated by Maginel Wright Enright. Introduction by Michael Patrick Hearn. Originally published under the pseudonym Laura Bancroft these six stories tell of the adventures of two children in Nature fairyland. xvi + 389 pp. 5 ½ x 7 ½. Price per copy $10.00(paperbound), $20.00 (clothbound, no jacket).

31. **Unexplored Territory in Oz** by pioneer Oz researcher Robert R. Pattrick. Four essays, 36 pp., 8 ½ x 11." Price per copy $3.00 (paperbound).

32. **Unexplored Territory In Oz** (Annotated) by Robert R. Pattrick. Four essays, plus annotations and additional essays by Patrick M. Maund. 56 pp. 8 ½ x 11." Price per copy, $4.00 (paperbound)

33. **Who's Who in Oz** by Jack Snow. Illustrations by John R. Neill, Frank Kramer, and Dirk. This book contains more than 630 written descriptions and more than 490 illustrations of Oz characters from the first 39 Oz books. In addition, there are plot summaries of these books and biographical sketches of their authors and illustrators. 178 pp. 9 x 7. Price per copy $16.00 (clothbound).

34.   **The Wizard of Way Up and Other Wonders** by Ruth Plumly Thompson. Illustrated by Marge and others. This book contains some of Ruth Plumly Thompson's finest writings including two short novels about the wizard of Way Up and his merry crew as well as poems and short stories which were originally printed in magazines and newspapers and which are now nearly inaccessible in their original form. 184 pp. 8 ½ x 5 ½. **SALE PRICE!** $6.00 (paperbound)

35.   **The Wizard of Oz in Pictures,** printed and illustrated by Peter and Donna Thomas. Follow the story of Baum's original <u>Wizard of Oz</u> in this magnificent miniature book handmade exclusively for the Club. Measuring approximately 1.75 by 3 inches and bound in blue gingham cloth, the book stretches accordion style to follow the highlights of the story along the yellow brick road. A custom yellow brick slipcover is included. Limited edition of 75 signed/numbered copies (lettered edition is already sold out). Price per copy $125.00.

36.   **The Wizard of Oz: The Screenplay.** Edited with an introduction by Michael Patrick Hearn. Price per copy $12.00 (paperbound)

THE BAUM BUGLE - COLLECTIONS AND BACK ISSUES

37.   **The Best of The Baum Bugle: 1957–1961**. This magazine contains material from the earliest days of the Oz Club. Writers include Frank Joslyn Baum, Harry Neal Baum, Ruth Plumly Thompson, and Edward Wagenknecht. One feature is A Murder in Oz, a short story by Jack Snow. 32 pp., 8 ½ x 11 Price per copy $4.00.

38.   **The Best of The Baum Bugle: 1961–1962**. This magazine contains material from the time when Dick Martin was editor of the Bugle. Writers include Harry Neal Baum, Russell MacFall, Ruth Plumly Thompson and Dick Martin. 116 pp., 8 ½ x 11." Price per copy $8.00.

39.   **The Best of The Baum Bugle: 1963–1964**. Included are features about W. W. Denslow and John R. Neill, articles about Oz maps and foreign editions of the Oz books, and stories by L. Frank Baum and W. W. Denslow. 100 pp., 8 ½ x 11." Price per copy $8.00.

40.   **The Best of The Baum Bugle: 1965–1966**. Writers include Matilda J. Gage, Ruth Plumly Thompson, Harry Neal Baum, and Dick Martin. Features include The Enchanted Tree of Oz by Ruth Plumly Thompson. 125 pp., 8 ½ x 11." Price per copy $12.00.

SPECIAL PUBLICATIONS

41. **The Best of The Baum Bugle: 1967–1968**. Material from the club's early days is still fresh and informative. Contents include L. Frank Baum's play The Fairy Prince, reprints of interviews with L. Frank Baum, and numerous photographs of Baum and his family. There are articles about The Laughing Dragon of Oz and its sequel, the Oz comic page of 1904-1905, and The Wizard of Oz stage play. Price per copy $12.00 (paperbound)

42. **The Best of The Baum Bugle: 1969-1970**. Cover Includes full color reproductions of the six original covers. Price per copy $12.00.

Back issues of **The Baum Bugle**, the journal of the International Wizard of Oz Club, are available in limited quantities. Please visit our website www.ozclub.org or inquire for available issues and general information.

All remittances must be in U.S. funds and should be either in the form of a check or money order, or can be made online at www.paypal.com (user ID "postmanofoz@aol.com"). Please make your check or money order payable to The International Wizard of Oz Club and mail to:

The International Wizard of Oz Club
Department E
1407 A Street, Suite D
Antioch, California 94509

Terms:

A. The prices listed are the retail prices.
B. Club members may subtract 20% from all prices.
C. Book dealer inquiries may be made to the above address or to postmanofoz@aol.com.
D. Books described as "cloth" are hardcover books with dust jacket, unless noted otherwise.
E. Shipping within the US $3.00 for the 1st item + $1.00 per additional item. Shipping to Canada is $6.00 for the 1st item + $2.00 per additional item. All other international shipping is $9.00 for the 1st item + $2.00 per additional item.

Membership to **The International Wizard of Oz Club** is only $25.00 per year ($35.00 for non-U.S. members), and includes a subscription to **The Baum Bugle**, discounts on products and publications, annual conferences, and other benefits. Premium membership levels are also available. Visit www.ozclub.org for more information.